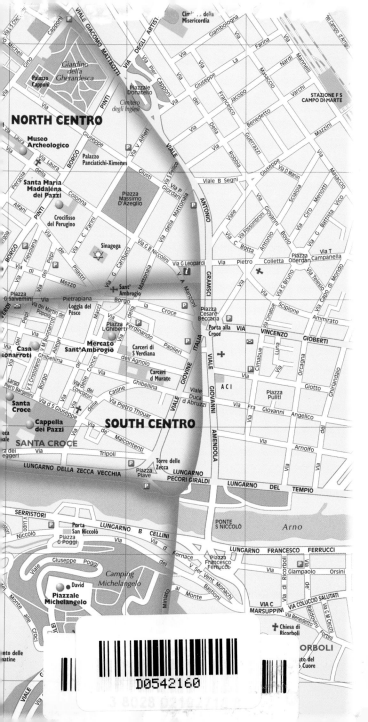

CITYPACK GUIDE TO
Florence

How to Use
This Book

KEY TO SYMBOLS

✚ Map reference to the accompanying fold-out map	❓ Other practical information
✉ Address	▷ Further information
☎ Telephone number	ℹ Tourist information
🕐 Opening/closing times	✋ Admission charges: Expensive (over €8), Moderate (€5–€8), and Inexpensive (under €5)
🍴 Restaurant or café	
🚃 Nearest rail station	★ Major Sight ★ Minor Sight
Ⓜ Nearest subway (Metro) station	👣 Walks 🚌 Excursions
🚌 Nearest bus route	🛍 Shops
⛴ Nearest riverboat or ferry stop	🎵 Entertainment and Nightlife
♿ Facilities for visitors with disabilities	🍴 Restaurants

This guide is divided into four sections
• Essential Florence: An introduction to the city and tips on making the most of your stay.
• Florence by Area: We've broken the city into four areas, and recommended the best sights, shops, entertainment venues, nightlife and restaurants in each one. Suggested walks help you to explore on foot.
• Where to Stay: The best hotels, whether you're looking for luxury, budget or something in between.
• Need to Know: The info you need to make your trip run smoothly, including getting about by public transport, weather tips, emergency phone numbers and useful websites.

Navigation In the Florence by Area chapter, we've given each area its own colour, which is also used on the locator maps throughout the book and the map on the inside front cover.

Maps The fold-out map accompanying this book is a comprehensive street plan of Florence. The grid on this fold-out map is the same as the grid on the locator maps within the book. We've given grid references within the book for each sight and listing.

Contents

CONTENTS

Introducing Florence

Florence, the Cradle of the Renaissance: This little city contributes so much to European culture through its paintings, harmonious *palazzi* that line the narrow streets, monumental civic buildings and splendid churches dominating spacious piazzas.

Getting around is easy. The core of the city is tiny and you can walk nearly everywhere, made more pleasant with the pedestrianization of the area from the Duomo south through Piazza della Signoria to the Ponte Vecchio and east from the Signoria to Santa Croce. However, the sheer number of tourists during peak times can make walking slow. Yet Florentines have no intention of killing the goose that lays the golden egg, and have poured money into doing whatever's possible to make the city visitor-friendly. Prices are high, but not too high. Hotels and restaurants provide what their customers want; museums have been revamped wherever possible; and shopping is taken seriously.

Florence should be a pleasure, not a cultural marathon. Try to concentrate on what you want to do, not what you think you should do. You might find more pleasure in exploring the quiet streets of the Oltrarno than standing in line for hours to jostle for two minutes in front of a Botticelli masterpiece. A picnic in the greenery of the Boboli Gardens may be more memorable than an overpriced pizza in a crowded bar. If you do want to saturate yourself with Renaissance art, plan ahead and reserve tickets.

You can also take advantage of the city's proximity to some of Italy's most beautiful countryside, a dreamy landscape of rolling hills dotted with villages and cypresses.

Even though every year sees a rise in visitors, the core of Florence retains the richness of its golden age and little has changed since the great construction works of the Renaissance. But it's up to you to get beneath the city's crowded surface to the beautiful heart below.

Facts + Figures

- Florence attracts around 6 million visitors a year.
- The native population is around 370,000.
- Florence has one of the lowest birth rates in Italy.
- The Uffizi Gallery is Italy's most visited museum—some 1.6 million visitors a year.

UFFIZI BOMBING

In May 1993 a huge bomb exploded on the west side of the Uffizi, killing five people, causing structural harm to the building, destroying the Gregoriophilus Library and damaging some 32 pictures, three of which were totally destroyed. Once thought to have been the work of the Mafia, the crime remains unsolved and the culprits have never been caught.

ON THE BALL

The Medici family, virtual sovereigns from the 14th to 18th centuries, left their mark on every building owned by or connected with them, so look out for their coat of arms, a varying number of balls *(palle)* on a shield, on buildings everywhere. The *palle* probably represent pills or coins, references to their original trade as apothecaries and later their role as bankers.

FLOOD FACTS

In November 1966 the River Arno burst its banks to disastrous effect: The tide, bludgeoning through the streets reached as high as 6m (20ft) in the Santa Croce region. This was not the only flood there has ever been, however: Bridges were swept away in 1269 and 1333, and the city was submerged in 1557 and 1884, but not as badly as in 1966.

A Short Stay in Florence

DAY 1

Morning Make an early start and head to the **Duomo** (▷ 58–59) to gaze on its mighty proportions; alongside are the superb **Campanile** (▷ 56) and **Battistero** (▷ 55). You can find out more about the history at the nearby **Museo dell'Opera del Duomo** (▷ 62). If you are feeling fit, climb to the top of either the Duomo or Campanile for great views of the city, but remember you will probably be jostling for space.

Mid-morning Take a coffee at one of the café-terraces along the traffic-free Piazza del Duomo to recharge your batteries. Head northwest up to **Mercato San Lorenzo** (▷ 68), the street market that sprawls around **San Lorenzo** (▷ 64). You'll find traders here selling everything from knitwear to jewellery. It's particularly known for its bargain leather goods—keep a look out for pickpockets and don't be afraid to haggle.

Lunch Right by the market is the unassuming **Gozzi Sergio** (▷ 75), renowned for its hearty Tuscan fare.

Afternoon Finish your shopping and then walk down Via Pucci and right into Via Ricasoli to the **Galleria dell'Accademia** (▷ 60–61) to view Michelangelo's massive masterpiece *David*. There's plenty more to see in the gallery, or you might prefer to backtrack and take in the **Palazzo Medici-Riccardi** (▷ 63).

Dinner For a special treat try **Hostaria Bibendum** (▷ 49) in the **Helvetia & Bristol** hotel in Via dei Pescioni (▷ 112). For a cheaper option there's **Belle Donne** (▷ 47), located close to **Via de' Tornabuoni** (▷ 36).

Evening Stroll down to the grandiose **Piazza della Repubblica** (▷ 39) with its triumphal arch, for a touch of Florentine atmosphere.

Morning Lines form from as early as 7am at the **Galleria degli Uffizi** (▷ 28–29), with its priceless paintings and sculptures, so get there as early as you can; be patient and you will be rewarded.

Mid-morning Just behind the Uffizi, relax with a coffee at **Rivoire** (▷ 50), the best and probably the most expensive café in **Piazza della Signoria** (▷ 32). Leave the piazza and turn left into Via Por Santa Maria and stroll over the **Ponte Vecchio** (▷ 34–35) to be dazzled by its jewellery shops. There are plenty more gift shops just over the bridge.

Lunch Grab a light lunch at the **Caffè Pitti** (▷ 91), opposite the entrance of the Palazzo Pitti.

Afternoon Take in the **Palazzo Pitti** (▷ 84–85). There are seven museums, plus the Royal Apartments to see, or if the weather is hot you might choose to stroll in the **Giardino di Boboli** (▷ 82). Be prepared for crowds. Then wander around the streets of Oltrarno and along to the church of Santa Maria del Carmine with the **Cappella Brancacci** (▷ 81) and its wonderful frescoes. This area has workshops, local shops and cafés. If you are feeling fit, cross over the bridge and walk along the riverfront to **Santa Croce** (▷ 33).

Dinner The Boccadama (▷ 47) wine bar-cum-restaurant is in a nice spot to appreciate the lively square of Santa Croce.

Evening If the weather is kind you can get a great view of the city after dark from **Piazzale Michelangelo** (▷ 87) in the southeast of Oltrarno. Catch bus 13 to get there. Alternatively, take bus 7 up to the hill town of **Fiesole** (▷ 97) for wonderful views of Florence illuminated at night.

Top 25

▶▶▶

Bargello ▷ 24–25
Overview of Florentine sculpture through works by Michelangelo, and others.

Battistero ▷ 55 One of Florence's oldest buildings, famous for its three sets of bronze doors.

Campanile ▷ 56 An incredible sight towering 85m (279ft) over the city, and offering great views.

Via de' Tornabuoni ▷ 36
The cream of world fashion is elegantly displayed on this street in the heart of medieval Florence.

Santissima Annunziata ▷ 67 Elegant, neoclassical arches grace the facade of this lovely church built by Michelozzo.

Santa Maria Novella ▷ 66 A great Florentine church full of superb artworks.

Santa Croce ▷ 33 The largest Franciscan church in Italy, incorporating the Cappella dei Pazzi. Galileo and Michaelangelo are buried here.

San Miniato al Monte ▷ 83 A fine Romanesque church perched on a hill with wonderful views.

San Marco ▷ 65
Beautiful convent where the paintings of Fra Angelico are a feast for the eyes.

San Lorenzo ▷ 64 This church is a superb example of archetypal Renaissance architecture.

Ponte Vecchio ▷ 34–35
One of the immediately recognizable emblems of Florence.

Piazza della Signoria ▷ 32 A traffic-free sculpture gallery with elegant cafés and restaurants.

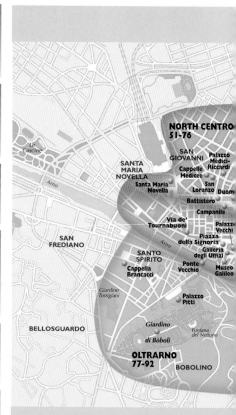

These pages are a quick guide to the Top 25, which are described in more detail later. Here they are listed alphabetically, and the tinted background shows which area they are in.

Cappella Brancacci ▷ 80 The chapel is covered from top to bottom with a monumental fresco cycle.

Cappella dei Pazzi ▷ 26 An early Renaissance masterpiece by Filippo Brunelleschi.

Cappelle Medicee ▷ 57 The Medici family's private chapels, visable proof of the dynasty's wealth.

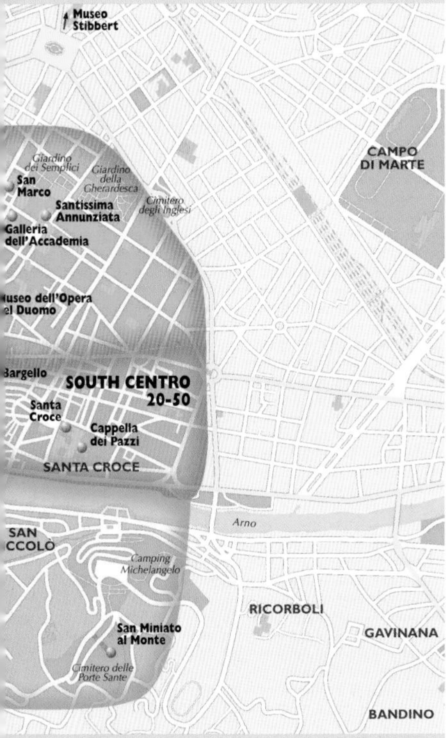

Museo Stibbert
Giardino dei Semplici
Giardino della Gherardesca
San Marco
Santissima Annunziata
Cimitero degli Inglesi
Galleria dell'Accademia
CAMPO DI MARTE
useo dell'Opera el Duomo
Bargello
SOUTH CENTRO 20-50
Santa Croce
Cappella dei Pazzi
SANTA CROCE
Arno
SAN CCOLÒ
Camping Michelangelo
RICORBOLI
San Miniato al Monte
GAVINANA
Cimitero delle Porte Sante
BANDINO

Duomo ▷ 58–59 A sublime masterpiece of Renaissance architecture with a mighty dome.

Fiesole ▷ 97 The perfect hilltop destination for a change from the city and its crowds.

Galleria degli Uffizi ▷ 28–29 One of Europe's oldest galleries to view Renaissance art.

Galleria dell'Accademia ▷ 60–61 Home to *David*, Michelangelo's world-famous sculpture.

Giardino di Boboli ▷ 82 A green space in the middle of Florence, a cool oasis on a hot summer's day.

Museo Galileo ▷ 27 The history of science brought to life with this fine collection.

Museo dell'Opera del Duomo ▷ 62 Home to the Duomo collection.

Palazzo Vecchio ▷ 30 The grand embodiment of Florentine civic purposes from the 14th century.

Palazzo Pitti ▷ 84–85 The city's largest and most opulent palace containing a fine picture collection.

Palazzo Medici-Riccardi ▷ 63 A massive palace, the residence of the Medici until 1540.

Shopping

Florence is high on every visiting shopper's itinerary, but it's also a big attraction for Italians, who rate it highly for leather goods, fabrics, bedlinen, lingerie, china and ceramics. As Tuscany's capital, Florence has the pick of Tuscan goods and shops, and people come from all over the region for a wider choice than they'll find at home. In the era of the global market, much of what's on sale is available worldwide, but the choice is wider and the prices often lower for many Italian essentials. Designer fashion also draws the crowds; one of Florence's many claims to fame is as the headquarters of Gucci (▷ 42).

Something to Take Home

The nicest souvenirs are often everyday items—kitchenware, household linen, tools and quirky stationery. Head for the markets for good value espresso coffee-makers and the tiny cups to go with them, and wonderful gadgets such as fish-scalers and plastic goods in vivid shades. Plastic also features heavily in the inexpensive and cheerful children's toys; the tiny shops away from the main streets often are the best value. Fresh produce and leather goods are also in plentiful supply in Florence's markets. Food is a popular take-home; you could consider more prosaic goods than expensive oils and

STREET TRADE

Street trading is an essential part of the Florentine scene, with tourists being offered everything from fake designer bags to lighters and African objects. Some traders are unlicensed and keep a constant eye open for approaching *carabinieri*, ready to scoop up their merchandise and run. The authorities are now clamping down on such practices. Red signs warning you to watch what you buy and beware of fakes are prominently displayed in central Florence. Throughout Italy purchases of counterfeited goods are punishable by law with fines of up to €10,000, and a policy of zero tolerance has been implemented. You have been warned!

Florence is the place to shop for shoes, designer names, culinary delights and toys

wine—how about herb packs specially blended for different foods, the excellent stock cubes known as *dadi* or sachets of vanilla sugar?

Traditional Crafts

One of Florence's major attractions is the wealth of artisan workshops, clustered mainly across the river in the Oltrarno area. Many specialize in antiques restoration for the city's numerous dealers, but there's more. Look for picture framers where you can get new purchases mounted, shoemakers selling wonderful velvet pads and brushes, and marble-paper makers where you may have a chance to watch the whole creative process.

Florence on View

Prints, books and old maps and city plans make special souvenirs, and there are cookbooks on Tuscan cuisine, many in English. Beautiful calendars with views of Florence are on sale as early as April for the following year. The museum shops are good for these, too.

Florentine Kitsch

There's no chance that you'll be overwhelmed by good taste either; there are T-shirts bearing images of Michelangelo and Botticelli, plastic models of the Duomo and Ponte Vecchio, umbrellas shaped like the Duomo, grotesque ceramics and fakes of every description. Where else could you buy such a blatant silvery reproduction of Michelangelo's *David*, complete with twinkling lights?

Something to take home—a bag from the market, herbs, or a fashionable accessory from a top Florentine name

---

ON A BUDGET

Markets are the best source of inexpensive and second-hand clothing with an Italian twist. The weekly Cascine market (▷ 98) is where locals go for bargains. The area around San Lorenzo is a great place for up-to-the-minute, inexpensive designs. The Mall (☎ 055 865 7775; www. themall.it), a 30-minute drive south of Florence at Leccio, has outlets for all the major top brands (twice daily bus service from Florence central bus station, at Via Santa Caterina di Siena 17).

Shopping by Theme

For a more detailed write-up of these shops, see Florence by Area.

ANTIQUES/PRINTS

Antichità Monna Agnese (▷ 102)
Baccani (▷ 41)
Bartolozzi & Maioli (▷ 89)
Bottega delle Stampe (▷ 89)
La Casa della Stampa (▷ 89)
Cornici Campani (▷ 71)
Ducci (▷ 42)
Giovanni Turchi (▷ 90)
Vanda Nencioni (▷ 44)

CERAMICS/PORCELAIN

Armando Poggi (▷ 41)
Arte Creta (▷ 71)
Bartolini (▷ 71)
La Botteghina (▷ 71)
Ceramiche Artisiche Santa Caterina (▷ 102)
Ceramiche di Sugarò (▷ 101)
Ceramisti d'Arté (▷ 101)
Galleria Ponte Vecchio (▷ 89)
Lenzi Ghino Giacomo (▷ 101)
Pampaloni (▷ 43)
Richard Ginori (▷ 73)
Sbigoli Terrecotte (▷ 73)

FASHION

Angela Caputi (▷ 41)
Anna (▷ 89)
Blunauta (▷ 71)
Coin (▷ 41)
Cortecci Abbigliamento (▷ 102)
Echo (▷ 72)
Emilio Cavallini (▷ 42)
Emilio Pucci (▷ 42)
Gucci (▷ 42)
Hermès (▷ 72)

Intimissimi (▷ 72)
J. T. Casini ▷ (90)
Luisa Via Roma (▷ 43)
Max & Co (▷ 43)
MaxMara (▷ 72)
Pitti Boutique (▷ 90)
Prada–Donna (▷ 44)
Raspini (▷ 73)
La Rinascente (▷ 44)
Roberto Cavalli (▷ 44)
Sisley (▷ 44)
Tessuti A Mano (▷ 102)

GOLD/JEWELLERY

Alcozer & J (▷ 89)
Bottega Orafa Penko (▷ 71)
Cassetti (▷ 41)
Fratelli Piccini (▷ 42)
The Gold Corner (▷ 42)
Ornamenta (▷ 72)
Parenti (▷ 43)

LEATHER/SHOES

A. Risaliti (▷ 41)
Il Bosonte (▷ 41)
Cellerini (▷ 41)
Fratelli Rossetti (▷ 42)
Furla (▷ 42)
Leather School (▷ 42)
Madova Gloves (▷ 90)
Martelli (▷ 43)
Misuri (▷ 43)
Rive Gauche (▷ 90)
Romano (▷ 44)
Salvatore Ferragamo (▷ 44)

LINEN/FABRICS

Antico Setificio Fiorentino (▷ 89)
Ermeni (▷ 72)
Frette (▷ 72)
Loretta Caponi (▷ 72)
Siena Ricama (▷ 102)
Valmar (▷ 44)

PHARMACISTS

Farmacia Molteni (▷ 42)
Farmacia Pitti (▷ 89)

STATIONERY/GIFTS

Abacus (▷ 71)
Alice's Masks Art Studio (▷ 71)
Bottega del Mosaico (▷ 89)
Fratelli Alinari (▷ 72)
Giulio Giannini e Figlio (▷ 90)
Letizia Fiorini (▷ 42)
Libreria Antiquaria Gonnelli (▷ 72)
Moleria Locchi (▷ 90)
Olfattorio (▷ 43)
Il Papiro (▷ 73)
Parione (▷ 43)
Le Pietre Nell'Arte (▷ 73)
Pineider (▷ 44)
Scriptorium (▷ 73)
Il Torchio (▷ 90)

WINE/FOOD

Arte del Cioccolato (▷ 41)
Borgo (▷ 71)
La Bottega della Frutta (▷ 41)
Caniparoli (▷ 101)
Casa del Vino (▷ 71)
Drogheria Manganelli (▷ 102)
Federico Salza (▷ 101)
Marsili Costantino (▷ 101)
Morbidi (▷ 102)
Olio & Convivium (▷ 90)
Osteria de l'Ortolano (▷ 72)
Pegna (▷ 43)
Per Bacco (▷ 43)
Taddeucci (▷ 101)
Terre dei Gigli (▷ 73)
Vinarius (▷ 44)
Zanobini (▷ 73)

ESSENTIAL FLORENCE SHOPPING BY THEME

12

Florence by Night

To kick off your evening and for a taste of local life don't miss the *passeggiata*. Year-round, this quintessentially Italian nightly ritual sees the streets thronged with hundreds of locals, out to see and be seen, while window-shopping and meeting friends.

An Evening Stroll

The best place to see the fashion peacocks in their finery is on Via dei Calzaiuoli, linking Piazza del Duomo with Piazza della Signoria. To enjoy a drink while you people-watch, go to Piazza della Repubblica, with its expensive cafés. After dinner, wander along the Lungarni, the name given to the streets beside the river. The Ponte Vecchio is just as crowded by night as by day.

Stunning by Night

Evening is the ideal time to admire Florentine architecture as the floodlighting enhances many buildings. Don't miss the Piazza della Signoria and the area between it and the Duomo. The private palazzi look superb at this time of day and you can peek into courtyards and loggias. Street entertainers add to the atmosphere.

Culture, Concerts and Clubbing

Florence has a year-round schedule of cultural evening events. The free monthly tourist magazine *Chiavi d'Oro Toscana* has full listings. Newspapers are another good source. *Firenze Spettacolo* also details everything that's on, including rock concerts, clubs and discos.

PICK OF THE PANORAMAS

A great evening vantage point is Piazzale Michelangelo (▷ 87), which gives a glorious panorama of the Duomo illuminated, Florence's twinkling lights and the misty hills beyond. The square draws the crowds during the day but things are quieter at night. There's a restaurant and a couple of bars if you want to spend the evening here; avoid the park/gardens area below the square at night. In late June, the square hosts the spectacular fireworks display celebrating the feast of San Giovanni.

A night out? Choose from a walk by the river, a concert in a church, or a drink in one of the city's historic bars

Eating Out

Eating is definitely one of life's pleasures in Florence, as it is all over Italy. The food is fresh, seasonal and, above all, local. You'll eat the best of Tuscan produce cooked to Tuscan recipes.

Mealtimes

If you are heading for breakfast in a bar, most open for business around 7–7.30. Restaurants normally open for lunch around 12.30 or 1 and stop serving at 3; they close for the afternoon and reopen for dinner around 7.30–8. The majority of restaurants have one closing day a week but many open every day in summer.

Where to Eat

Trattorie are usually family-run places and are generally more basic than restaurants. Sometimes there is no written menu and the waiter will reel off the list of the day's specials. They normally open for lunch and in the evening. *Ristoranti* are not always open for lunch. The food and surroundings are usually more refined than those of a trattoria. Both, however, add a cover charge, which includes bread, and a service charge to the bill. *Pizzerie* specialize in pizzas, but often serve simple pasta dishes as well. Look out for *forno al legno*—pizzas cooked in a wood-fired oven. *Osterie* can either be old-fashioned places specializing in home-cooked food or extremely elegant, long-established restaurants.

PAYING THE BILL

Pay by requesting the bill (*il conto*), and check to see whether service is included. Scribbled bills on scraps of paper are illegal; if you don't get a proper one, say that you need a receipt (*una recevuta*), which all restaurants, bars and shops are legally obliged to issue. Both they and you can be fined if you do not take this with you. Some smaller establishments expect to be paid in cash but you'll be able to use a credit card in most establishments. If service is included, it's customary to leave a small tip— some loose change will do.

Italian cuisine Florentine-style. It's morning coffee, ice cream, wine and pasta that will stay in the memory

Restaurants by Cuisine

There are restaurants to suit all tastes and budgets in Florence. On this page they are listed by cuisine. For a more detailed description of each restaurant, see Florence by Area.

If You Like…

However you'd like to spend your time in Florence, these top suggestions should help you tailor your ideal visit. Each suggestion has a fuller write-up elsewhere in the book.

EXCLUSIVE SHOPPING

Descend on Via de' Tornabuoni (▷ 36) for the best in designer names—Armani, Gucci, Prada.
Sparkling gold and exquisite jewellery line either side of the Ponte Vecchio (▷ 34–35).
Florence is famed for its superb Italian shoes, and one of the best is Salvatore Ferragamo (▷ 44); you can visit the museum, too (▷ 38).

TAKING A SOUVENIR HOME

Stationery—Pineider (▷ 44) has the most gorgeous array of handmade paper and bound notebooks, plus pens and desk accessories.
Ceramics—choose an authentic jug or pot (▷ 89) from the large selection at the Galleria Ponte Vecchio.
Wine—all price ranges for the local Tuscan Chianti from Casa del Vino (▷ 71).

If you want to capture the true essence of Florence try all things local and take something home

EATING LOCAL CUISINE

Sit at a shared table, trying out local dishes, at Belle Donne (▷ 47).
The cuisine is Tuscan, the restaurant traditional—try Coco Lezzone (▷ 48) for that classic meal.
Close to the bridge of the same name, try Trattoria Ponte Vecchio (▷ 50).

HISTORIC CAFES

Gilli (▷ 48)—watch the world go by in the Piazza della Repubblica.
Paszkowski (▷ 50)—more indulgence on the Piazza della Reppublica—try the fruit tarts.
Rivoire (▷ 50)—set in the attractive Piazza Signoria, it's perfect to unwind in.

Italian ice cream at its best uses local produce and the freshest of ingredients

INDULGING IN ICE CREAM

You'll have difficulty deciding what to choose at Perché No! (▷ 50).

For delicious granitas and their special fruity *cremolata* visit Gelateria Carabé (▷ 75).

The most famous gelateria in Florence, Vivoli (▷ 50), changes its specials to suit the seasons.

A ROOM WITH A VIEW

Try the Hermitage (▷ 110) with its roof garden overlooking the River Arno.

For a panoramic bird's-eye view of the rooftops of Florence, head to the beautiful Palazzo Guadagni hotel (▷ 109) in the Oltrarno.

Some of the best views of the Tuscan countryside are from the hilltop town of Fiesole (▷ 97); for luxury as well try Villa San Michele (▷ 112).

SPLASHING OUT

Stay in the Helvetia & Bristol (▷ 112) for sheer luxury and elegance.

Shop in Via de' Tornabuoni (▷ 36) and stock your wardrobe with the top names in design.

Treat yourself to a refined cup of coffee at the stylish Paszkowski (▷ 50).

Stationery has been made in Florence for centuries (above); Italian fashion at its best (below)

PUTTING A SMILE ON THE KIDS' FACES

The Museo Stibbert (▷ 98) has a fine collection of armour for your budding knights.

Go to the soccer stadium (▷ 104) to cheer on local team Fiorentina when they're at home.

If you need to cool off, visit the Piscina le Pavoniere (▷ 104) outdoor pool.

FLORENCE ON A BUDGET

Ring the bell for a legendary cocktail

For good value combined with historic surroundings stay at the hotel Chiazza (▷ 109).
If the real thing is a bit pricey, there are some great lookalike bargains at San Lorenzo market (▷ 68).
There's no charge to see the stunning paintings in the church of Santa Felicita (▷ 87).

THE CITY BY NIGHT

Sip a cocktail in the world-famous nightspot, Harry's Bar (▷ 46).
Take a trip up to Piazzale Michelangelo (▷ 87) to view the city in all its glory at night.
Attend a concert or opera at Florence's largest concert hall, Teatro Comunale. (▷ 74).

A LAZY MORNING

Relax over breakfast on the roof garden of a hotel such as the Hermitage (▷ 110).
Amble across to the Boboli Gardens (▷ 82), a cool oasis on a hot summer's day and just the spot for a picnic.
Take refuge in the calm and tranquillity of Santa Maria Maddelena dei Pazzi (▷ 69).

TO DO SOMETHING DIFFERENT

Try your luck on the horses at the Ippodromi Fiorentini (▷ 104). Trotting races take place here as well.

There are plenty of green spaces in the city where you can relax

Hop on a bus and venture out to see some of Tuscany's hill towns or easily accessible Fiesole (▷ 97).
Be uplifted at a recital in one of Florence's splendid churches such as Santa Maria de' Ricci (▷ 46).

It doesn't take long to find a view in Florence, particularly from the top of a church such as San Miniato al Monte

Florence by Area

THE SOUTH CENTRO

THE NORTH CENTRO

OLTRARNO

FURTHER AFIELD

The South Centro

This district is the very heart of historic Florence. Its pedestrianized, cobbled streets and wide piazzas are a joy. Here, too, are fine Renaissance palaces and the ancient grid of medieval lanes.

3

4

5

IL PRATO BORCO

Via Montebello

Via Maso Finiguerra

Via della SCALA

P

Ognissanti

Palazzo Lenzi

Hercules

Piazza Ognissanti

Ospedale di San Giovanni di Dio

VESPUCCI

LUNGARNO AMERICO

PONTE A VESPUCCI

Via del Porcellana

Via del Palazzuolo

Via della Spada

Via del Sole

Via della Vigna Nuova

Museo Marino Marini

Palazzo Rucellai

Piazza Santa Maria Novella

Via delle Belle Donne

VIA DE FOSSI

VIA DEL

VIA DE' TORNABUONI

VIA DEL TREBBIO

Via dei Banchi

Via degli Agli

Via del Campidoglio

Via de' Pecori

Via de' Rondinelli

Via delle Pescioni

Piazza della Repubblica

Via degli Strozzi

Via degli Anselmi

Via Calzaiuoli

Via de' Oche

Casa di Dante

San Martino del Vescovo

Orsanmichele

Badia Fiorentina

Via Dante Alighieri

Palazzo Firenze

Palazzo Strozzi

Palazzo Davanzati

Via de' Tornabuoni

Via del Parione

Piazza Goldoni

Palazzo Corsini

Via di Vigna Nuova

Santa Trinita

Colonna della Giustizia

Piazza di Santa Trinita

PONTE ALLA CARRAIA

LUNGARNO CORSINI

LUNGARNO ACCIAIUOLI

Porta Rossa

Via Monalda

Mercato Nuovo

Museo Salvatore Ferragamo

Santi Apostoli

S. Stefano

Via Porta Rossa

Via Condotta

Piazza della Signoria

Galleria degli Uffizi

Museo Galileo

Palazzo Vecchio

Via de' Castellani

Palazzo Vita

Piazza Menta

Ponte Santa Trinita

Ponte Vecchio

LUNGARNO ARCHIBUSIERI

L MEDICI

LUNGARNO G

Arno

6

7

8

0 — 250 m

0 — 250 yds

D **E** **F**

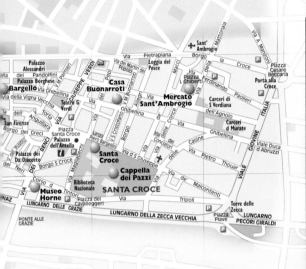

Palazzo
Alessandri
Palazzo Borghese
la   dei   Pandolfini
Bargello
Via Ghibellina
Via della Vigna Vecchia
dell'   Anguillara
San Firenze
Borgo dei Greci
Palazzo dei
Da Diaceto
dei   Neri

**Casa
Buonarroti**

Teatro G
Verdi

Via dei Martiri del
Popolo
Via
Pietrapiana

**Loggia del
Pesce**

Via dei

Via S Cristoforo
Via M Buonarroti
Borgo
Via Ghibellina
Via
Alighieri
Piazza
Santa Croce
Largo
Piero Bargellini
Via di S Giuseppe
Via delle Conce
Via dei
Conciatori
Via delle Casine

Piazza
Santa Croce
Palazzo
dell'Antella

**Santa
Croce**

**Cappella
dei Pazzi**

Via Pietro Thouar
Via de' Malcontenti

Biblioteca
Nazionale
SANTA CROCE

**Museo
Horne**
LUNGARNO DELLE GRAZIE
Piazza dei
Cavalleggeri

Via

Tripoli

PONTE ALLE
GRAZIE
LUNGARNO DELLA ZECCA VECCHIA

Sant'
Ambrogio
Borgo   la   Croce

**Mercato
Sant'Ambrogio**

Via dei Pilastri
Piazza
L Ghiberti

Via Ferdinando Paoletti

Carceri di
S Verdiana
dell'Agnolo

Carceri
d Murate
Ghibellina

Casine

Plaza
Cesare
Beccaria
**Porta alla
Croce**

Via A Manzoni
Via Mattonaia
Via G Carducci

VIALE GIOVINE ITALIA

Viale Duca
d Abruzzi

**Torre delle
Zecca**
Piazza
Piave
LUNGARNO
PECORI GIRALDI

G   H   J

Bargello

HIGHLIGHTS

- Donatello's *David*
- Giambologna's *Mercury*
- Giambologna's animals
- Michelangelo's *Bacchus*
- Della Robbia's terracottas
- Courtyard

TIP

- The museum is very popular and in high season it is best to book in advance.

The Bargello, with its airy courtyard, is so pleasant that you would want to visit it even if it were not home to what is arguably the finest collection of Renaissance sculpture in the world.

Diverse uses Built in 1255, the Bargello was the first seat of Florence's city government and served as the city's main law court before being passed to the *Bargello* (Chief of Police) in 1574; it was used as a prison until 1859. In 1865 it opened as a museum, with an unrivalled collection of Renaissance sculpture and decorative arts.

Courtyard art The courtyard walls, once the site of executions, carry the coats of arms of the *Podestà* (chief magistrates), whose headquarters were here, and 16th-century sculpture, including

Clockwise from left: The Bargello viewed from the Campanile; inside the vaulted Bargello; the plaque of Christina de' Medici; a bust of Piero di Lorenzo di Medici; the striking facade of the Bargello; a stained-glass crest; the arcaded courtyard

Giambologna's *Oceanus* from the Boboli Gardens (▷ 82). The ground floor has important works by Michelangelo, Cellini and Giambologna, including *Mercury* (1564).

Sculpture, medals and bronzes In the Salone del Consiglio Generale, a vaulted hall on the first floor that was once the courtroom, works by Donatello include his decidedly camp bronze *David* (c.1430–40), dressed in long boots and a jaunty hat (the first freestanding nude since the Roman period), and his *St. George* (1416), sculpted for the exterior of Orsanmichele (▷ 39). On the second floor, enamel terracottas by the della Robbia family include the bust of a boy by Andrea della Robbia. Note the displays of Italian medals and small Renaissance bronzes. The arms room has ivory-inlay saddles, guns and armour.

THE BASICS

www.polomuseale.firenze.it

🔒 G6

✉ Via del Proconsolo 4

☎ 055 294 883

🕐 Daily 8.15–2; closed 1st, 3rd, 5th Sun, 2nd, 4th Mon of month and 1 Jan, 1 May, 25 Dec

🚍 C1, C2

♿ Good

🎫 Moderate

Cappella dei Pazzi

TOP 25

Monochrome interior of the Cappella dei Pazzi (left); the serene cloisters and chapel (right)

THE BASICS

✚ H6
✉ Piazza Santa Croce
☎ 055 246 6105
🕐 Mon–Sat 9–5, Sun 2–5.30
🚌 C1, C2, C3
♿ Good
💰 Moderate; joint ticket with Santa Croce and Museo dell'Opera
❓ Access is through Santa Croce

HIGHLIGHTS

● Cappella dei Pazzi
● Cloister
● Roundels of the evangelists
● Cimabue's crucifix (13th century)
● Taddeo Gaddi's fresco (1333)
● Donatello's *St. Louis of Toulouse* (1424)
● Museo dell'Opera

In contrast to the adjacent church of Santa Croce, a key stop on the tourist circuit, the cloisters are not much visited. The solitude is perfect for appreciating their grace and harmony.

Convent building On the south side of Santa Croce are the buildings of a former convent. These include the Cappella dei Pazzi, one of the great architectural masterpieces of the early Renaissance, and a 14th-century refectory, which houses the Museo dell'Opera di Santa Croce. This is one of the lowest areas in Florence, and to the left of the Cappella dei Pazzi a plaque almost 6m (20ft) up shows the high point of the November 1966 floodwaters. The second cloister, a haven of calm, was designed by Filippo Brunelleschi.

The Pazzi Chapel The Cappella, which was commissioned as a chapter house by Andrea dei Pazzi and designed by Brunelleschi (*c.*1430), is incorporated into the cloisters. This domed chapel is done in *pietra serena* (grey sandstone) against a white plaster background, embellished only by enamel terracotta roundels.

Small but beautiful The museum contains many important works, including a restored crucifix by Giovanni Cimabue. On the walls a huge fresco by Taddeo Gaddi shows the Last Supper, the Tree of Life, St. Louis of Toulouse, St. Francis, St. Benedict and Mary Magdalene washing Christ's feet. Prominent is the gilded bronze statue of St. Louis of Toulouse (1424), sculpted by Donatello.

Scientific instruments (left); the astrolabe of the Gualtiero Arsenio (right)

A total revamp in 2010 brought this fascinating museum into the 21st century, with state-of-the-art themed exhibits putting Florence and Tuscany firmly among the major players in the development of science. Pick up one of the excellent audio-visual guides to get the best from your visit.

Pure science Focussing on imaginatively displayed scientific and mathematical instruments, the museum traces the role played by Florence in the development of modern science. Its core collection, dating from 1775, was acquired largely by the Medici Grand Dukes and has been displayed in the 14th-century Palazzo Castellani since 1929.

The Medici and Galileo Galilei The role of the Medici, Florence's dynastic ruling family from the 14th to the 18th centuries, in scientific study is appraised via scientific instruments, clocks, barometers and telescopes, and there is a fascinating section devoted to maps, globes and navigation. Look out in particular for the sumptuous armillary sphere, used to divine the movements of the planets, made for the Medici in 1590. Pisa-born scientist Galileo (1564–1642), gets star billing, with his telescopes, lenses and compasses on display—there is even a reliquary containing his finger bones.

More to see Upstairs you'll find precision instruments, automata and anatomical waxworks; a gruesome but compellingly fascinating spectacle.

THE BASICS

www.museogalileo.it
🟦 F6
✉ Piazza dei Guidici 1
☎ 055 265 311
🕐 Wed–Mon 9.30–6, Tue 9.30–1; closed public holidays
🚌 C3
♿ Excellent
✋ Expensive
❓ Excellent guide book

HIGHLIGHTS

● Galileo's telescope
● Lopo Homem's map of the world (16th century)
● Antonio Santucci's armillary sphere (1573)
● Copy of Lorenzo della Volpaia's clock of the planets (1593)

Galleria degli Uffizi

HIGHLIGHTS

● The Tribune (room 18)
● Giotto's *Ognissanti Madonna* (1310)
● Botticelli's *Birth of Venus* (1485) and *Primavera* (*c.*1480)
● Piero della Francesca's *Federico da Montefeltro and Battista Sforza* (1460)
● Leonardo's *Annunciation* (1472–75) and *Adoration of the Magi* (1481)
● Michelangelo's *Holy Family* (1508)
● Titian's *Venus of Urbino* (1538)

TIPS

● Reserve in advance; waiting can be up to 3 hours.
● Plan what you want to see as backtracking is difficult.
● Be patient, highlights are often blocked by large groups.
● There are frequent long waits for the toilet, so go before you arrive.

The Uffizi encompasses the artistic developments of the Renaissance and beyond. It is a powerful expression of Florence's extraordinary role in the history of art.

Medici art The gallery contains part of the Medici's art collection, bequeathed in 1737 by Anna Maria Luisa. The building was designed by Vasari, in the 1560s, as the administrative offices (*uffizi*) of the Grand Duchy. Parts of the building and collection that were damaged by the 1993 bomb were restored and reopened in 1998.

From sculpture to painting Today people come for the paintings, but until the 19th century the attraction was sculpture (mostly now in the Bargello, ▷ 24–25). The collection is displayed in chronological order, starting with the first stirrings

Clockwise from left: Detail of Filippo Lippi's Madonna with Child and Two Angels in the Uffizi; crowds gather outside the Uffizi; The Holy Family by Michelangelo; the gallery seen from the River Arno; the Corridoio Vasariano, linking the Uffizi with the Palazzo Pitti, crossing the Ponte Vecchio; artisitic magnificence in the gallery

of the Renaissance in the 13th century and ending with works by Caravaggio, Rembrandt and Canaletto from the 17th and 18th centuries. Uccello's *Battle of San Romano* (1456) exemplifies the technical advances of the Renaissance, while Filippo Lippi's *Madonna with Child and Two Angels* (c.1465) reveals the emotional focus typical of the period.

Venus Perhaps most fascinating is the Tribune, an octagonal chamber with a mother-of-pearl ceiling. In the middle is the Medici *Venus*, whose sensuous derrière earned her the reputation of the sexiest sculpture of the ancient world. Portraits include Bronzino's *Giovanni de Medici* (c.1549), a smiling boy holding a goldfinch. The café provides a welcome pitstop and has superb views of Piazza della Signoria.

THE BASICS

www.polo.museale.firenze.it

✚ F6

✉ Loggiato degli Uffizi 6

☎ 055 238 8651 (reserve ahead to avoid lines by calling 055 294 833 or online at www.firenzemusei.it)

🕐 Tue–Sun 8.15–6.50 (last admission 45 min before closing); closed 1 Jan, 1 May, 25 Dec

🍴 Cafe 🚌 C1, C2

♿ Good 💰 Expensive

Palazzo Vecchio

The striking Palazzo Vecchio, dominating the skyline, has many intricate details within

THE BASICS

www.museicivicifiorentini.comune.fi.it

F6

✉ Piazza della Signoria

☎ 055 276 8325

🕐 Apr–Sep Fri–Wed 9–midnight, Thu 9–2; Oct–Mar Fri–Wed 9–7, Thu 9–2

🚌 C1, C2

♿ Good

💰 Expensive

HIGHLIGHTS

● Sala delle Carte
● Sala dei Gigli
● Michelangelo's *Genius of Victory*
● Donatello's *Judith and Holofernes*
● View from the Terrazza di Saturno
● Salone dei Cinquecento

With its fortresslike castellations and its commanding 95m (311ft) bell tower, the Palazzo Vecchio conveys a message of political power supported by solid military strength.

Town Hall The Palazzo Vecchio is still Florence's town hall, as it has been since its completion by Arnolfo di Cambio in 1302. It was substantially renovated for Duke Cosimo I, who made it his palace in 1540. It became known as the Palazzo Vecchio (Old Palace) when Cosimo transferred his court to the Palazzo Pitti. During the brief period when Florence was the capital of Italy (1865–71), it housed the Parliament and Foreign Ministry.

Assembly room The vast Salone dei Cinquecento is 53.5m by 22m (175ft by 72ft), 18m (59ft) high and was designed in the 1490s, during the era of the Florentine Republic, as the meeting place of the 500-strong ruling assembly. Vasari painted the military scenes of Florence's victory over Siena and Pisa (1563–65). The theme of Florence's might is underscored by Michelangelo's *Genius of Victory* (1533–34), as well as sculptures of the *Deeds of Hercules* by Vincenzo dei Rossi.

Loggia views On the second floor the Terrazza di Saturno is an open loggia with views to the hills. The Sala dei Gigli is decorated with gold fleurs-de-lys and houses Donatello's *Judith and Holofernes* (1456–60). The Sala delle Carte (Map Room), has a wonderful collection of globes and maps painted on leather, showing the world in 1563.

Piazza della Signoria

The Piazza Signoria is a gathering place— from protests to costumed parades

THE BASICS

🞣 F6

✉ Piazza della Signoria

🚌 C1, C2

♿ Good

HIGHLIGHTS

● Loggia dei Lanzi (1376)
● Cellini's *Perseus* (1554)
● Giambologna's *Rape of the Sabine Women* (1583)
● Ammannati's *Neptune* (1575)
● Rivoire café
● Sorbi newspaper and postcard kiosk

Standing in the Piazza della Signoria in the shadow of the forbidding Palazzo Vecchio, it is impossible to escape the sense of Florence's past political might.

Political piazza The Piazza della Signoria has been the hub of political life in Florence since the 14th century. It was the scene of great triumphs, such as the return of the Medici in 1530, but also of the Bonfire of the Vanities instigated by Savonarola, who was himself burned at the stake here in 1498, denounced as a heretic by the Inquisition.

Significant sculptures The sculptures here bristle with political connotations, many of them fiercely contradictory. Michelangelo's *David* (the original is in the Accademia) was placed outside the Palazzo Vecchio as a symbol of the Republic's defiance of the tyrannical Medici. The *Neptune* (1575), by Ammannati, celebrates the Medici's maritime ambitions, and Giambologna's statue of Duke Cosimo I (1595), the man who brought all of Tuscany under Medici military rule. The statue of Perseus holding Medusa's head, by Cellini (1554), is a stark reminder of what happened to those who crossed the Medici. The graceful Loggia dei Lanzi, which functions as an open-air sculpture gallery, was designed by Orcagna in 1376.

Postcard paradise Sorbi, the newspaper kiosk, has an unrivalled collection of postcards and newspapers, which you could enjoy over a drink in the Rivoire café (▷ 50).

Aerial view of Santa Croce (left); detail of frescoes by Giotto in Santa Croce (right)

Santa Croce

Despite its vast size and swarms of tourists, Santa Croce is personal and touchingly intimate, perhaps because of the sense that one somehow knows the people buried here.

Burial place Santa Croce, rebuilt for the Franciscan order in 1294 by Arnolfo di Cambio, is the burial place of the great and the good in Florence. Michelangelo is buried in Santa Croce, as are Rossini, Machiavelli and the Pisa-born Galileo Galilei, who was excommunicated during the Inquisition and was not allowed a Christian burial until 1737, 95 years after his death. There is also a memorial to Dante, whose sarcophagus is empty.

Anglophile The church exterior is covered with a polychrome marble facade added in 1863 and paid for by the English benefactor Sir Francis Sloane. It overlooks the Piazza Santa Croce, site of an annual football game in medieval costume.

Artistic riches The artistic wealth in Santa Croce is stunning; frescoes by Gaddi (1380) in the Cappella Maggiore tell the story of the holy cross ('Santa Croce') and beautiful frescoes by Giotto in the Bardi and Peruzzi chapels show scenes from the lives of St. Francis and St. John the Evangelist. Don't miss the memorial to 19th-century playwright Giovanni Battista Nicolini, left of the entrance facing the altar, said to have inspired the Statue of Liberty. Santa Croce was severely hit by flooding in 1966, and you can still see a tide mark showing far up on the pillars and walls.

THE BASICS

www.santacroceopera.it
H6
Piazza Santa Croce
055 246 6105
Mon–Sat 9.30–5, Sun 2–5; closed during services
C1, C2, C3
Good
Expensive

HIGHLIGHTS

● Giotto's frescoes (1320–25)
● Tombs of Michelangelo, Machiavelli, Galileo
● Painted wooden ceiling
● Donatello's *Annunciation* (1435)
● Polychrome marble facade (1863)
● Wooden crucifix by Donatello
● 14th-century windows

Ponte Vecchio

TOP
25

HIGHLIGHTS

● Gold and jewellery shops
● Views of the Arno
● *Corridoio Vasariano* (1565)
● Bust of Cellini (1900)

TIP

● The sun sets directly downriver from the bridge, and the golden tones of the structure itself are magical on a good evening.

No visit to Florence is complete without a saunter down this bridge; lined with old shops jutting precariously over the water, it is difficult to believe you're on a proper bridge and not just strolling down a narrow street.

The test of time Near the Roman crossing, the Old Bridge was, until 1218, the only bridge across the Arno in Florence. The current bridge was rebuilt after a flood in 1345. During World War II, it was the only bridge the Germans did not destroy but they blocked access by demolishing the medieval buildings either side. On 4 November 1966 the bridge survived when the Arno burst its banks.

Private path When the Medici moved from the Palazzo Vecchio to the Palazzo Pitti, they decided

Clockwise from left: The vaulted arcades of the Ponte Vecchio were rebuilt by Michelozzo; gold has been sold on the Ponte Vecchio for centuries; detail of a section of the bridge; the Ponte Veccchio at dusk; bust of the sculptor, soldier and goldsmith Benvenuto Cellini guarding the bridge

they needed a connecting route from the Uffizi to the Palazzo Pitti on the other side of the river that enabled them to keep out of contact with their people. The result was Vasari's *Corridoio Vasariano*, built in 1565 on top of the buildings lining the bridge's eastern parapet.

Glitz Shops have been on the Ponte Vecchio since the 13th century: Initially all types—butchers and fishmongers and later tanners, whose industrial waste caused a pretty rank stench. In 1593 Medici Duke Ferdinand I decreed that only goldsmiths and jewellers be allowed on the bridge. When the shops close their wooden shutters it makes them look like suitcases. As one of the places that Florentines regularly come to for the *passeggiata*, it is also always full of Senegalese street vendors, hawking fake goods.

Via de' Tornabuoni

History meets style on the smartest street in town

THE BASICS

- ✚ E5–E6
- ✉ Via de' Tornabuoni
- 🚆 C2
- ♿ Good

HIGHLIGHTS

- Sassetti Chapel frescoes in Santa Trinità
- Ferragamo shoe museum
- Designer shops
- Palazzo Strozzi
- 17th-century facade of San Gaetano

Florence maybe one of the world's richest cultural cities, but it's also a place for serious shopping. Fashionable Via de' Tornabuoni supports the top names in fashion, set among the stunning palaces.

Shopping in palaces Italy has always been synonymous with style, think Milan or Rome, but Florence contributes in its own way, too. The city hosted Italy's earliest fashion shows in the 1950s, and innovative designers made their fortunes within the city's medieval palaces here on Via de' Tornabuoni. Salvatore Ferragamo, the flagship store and shoe museum (▷ 38), can be found within the Palazzo Spini Feroni, one of the best preserved private medieval palaces in Florence; while Guccio Gucci picked this street—three generations ago—for his headquarters, which is still based at 73r Tornabuoni. You may be intent on a bargain but spare a moment to glance up at the facades and interiors of the imposing buildings.

Beyond the shops At the north end of the street is the stunning Palazzo Antinori (1465), next to the city's greatest baroque church, San Gaetano (1648), a tranquil spot to escape the crowds. Halfway down is the impressive Palazzo Strozzi. At the end is Piazza Santa Trinità with its artistically rich church. Central to the square is the tall Column of Justice, brought from the Baths of Caracalla in Rome and given to Cosimo I in 1560 by Pope Pius IV. Just beyond here is the Santa Trinità Bridge (▷ 39) that links elegant Tornabuoni with Oltrarno on the south bank of the River Arno.

More to See

BADIA FIORENTINA

The Badia Fiorentina, the oldest monastery in Florence, was founded in AD978 by Willa, widow of Umberto, Margrave of Tuscany. It is best known in connection with the medieval poet, Dante, who used to meet Beatrice here. Its magnificent bell tower is Gothic at the top and Romanesque at the base. Inside are two works: Filippino Lippi's *The Madonna Appearing to St. Bernard*, left of the entrance, and the tomb of Count Ugo, son of Willa and Umberto.

➕ G6 ✉ Via del Proconsolo ☎ 055 264 402 🕐 Mon 3–6 🚆 C2 ♿ Impossible 💷 Free

CASA BUONARROTI

www.casabuonarroti.it

This house, which Michelangelo bought in 1508, is now a fascinating museum and gallery. Exhibits include the artist's earliest known work, the *Madonna della Scala* (c.1491), a wood and wax model (the only one of its type) of a river god, and a model of the facade for San Lorenzo never executed.

➕ H6 ✉ Via Ghibellina 70 ☎ 055 241 698 or 055 241 752 🚆 C2 🕐 Wed–Mon 9.30–5. Guided tours can be reserved ♿ Poor 💷 Expensive

CASA DI DANTE

www.museocasadidante.it

The 13th-century House of Dante has been restored and contains material relating to the author's life and work.

➕ F6 ✉ Via Santa Margherita 1 ☎ 055 219 416 🕐 Apr–Sep daily 10–6; Oct–Mar Tue–Sun 10–5 🚆 C1, C2 ♿ None 💷 Moderate

MERCATO NUOVO

So-called to distinguish it from the Mercato Vecchio, which closed in the 16th-century, this market is famous for the brass boar with a well-stroked nose, *Il Porcellino*, that sometimes lends its name to the market. It is also known as the 'straw market', a reference to the straw hats once sold here.

➕ F6 ✉ Loggiato del Porcellino, Via Porta Rossa 🕐 Mid-Mar to Oct daily 9–8; Nov to mid-Mar Tue–Sun 9–7.30 🚆 C1, C2 ♿ Good (but crowded)

The ceiling of the Badia Fiorentina is decorated with beautiful 15th-century frescoes

A popular pig in the Mercato Nuovo

MERCATO DI SANT'AMBROGIO

After the Mercato Centrale, this is the second most important market for fresh produce in Florence. It attracts Florence's working population, is inexpensive and is pleasantly noisy.

✚ H6 ✉ Piazza Lorenzo Ghiberti
🕐 Mon–Sat 7–2 🚌 C2, C3 ♿ Good

MUSEO HORNE

www.museohorne.it

This small museum, housed in Palazzo Corsi, owes its existence to the English art historian and collector Herbert Percy Horne (1864–1916). Horne bought the palazzo in 1904 for his interesting collection of paintings, furniture and sculpture. On his death, he left the palazzo and its contents to Italy.

✚ G7 ✉ Via de' Benci 6 ☎ 055 244 661
🕐 Mon–Sat 9–1; closed public hols 🚌 23, B, C ♿ None 💰 Moderate

MUSEO SALVATORE FERRAGAMO

www.museoferragamo.it

Founded in 1995, this collection of 10,000 pairs of shoes by Ferragamo dates from his return from Hollywood to Florence in 1927 until his death in the 1960s. The collection highlights Ferragamo's choice of hues, his imaginative models and experimentation with materials. Many examples were created for celebrities.

✚ E6 ✉ Palazzo Spini Feroni, Via de' Tornabuoni 2 ☎ 055 356 2417
🕐 Daily 10–7.30 🚌 C3, 6 ♿ Poor
💰 Moderate

OGNISSANTI

This was the parish church of the Vespucci family, and of Botticelli's family; he was buried here. In the second chapel on the right facing the altar is a fresco by Ghirlandaio, which is said to include Amerigo's portrait (the boy behind the Virgin). In the convent's *cenacolo* (refectory) there are more Ghirlandaio pieces—*The Last Supper* and *St. Jerome in his Study*—and Botticelli's *St. Augustine in his Study*.

✚ D5 ✉ Borgo Ognissanti 42 ☎ 055 239 8700 🕐 Daily 7–12.30, 4–8. *Last Supper* in convent Mon, Tue, Sat 9–12 🚌 C3, D
♿ Poor 💰 Free

An emblem on the Church of the Ognissanti (left); magnificent 17th- and 18th-century frescoes adorn the ceiling and walls of the Ognissanti (right)

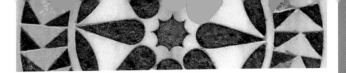

ORSANMICHELE

Built as a grain market in 1337, Orsanmichele became a church in 1380. The city's guilds commissioned some of the best artists to make statues of patron saints to sit in the canopied niches, and so created a permanent outdoor exhibition of 15th-century Florentine sculpture. These statues are being removed one by one for restoration and copies put in their place. Some of the original works are still there, including Lorenzo Ghiberti's bronzes of St. Matthew (1419–22). A museum opened here in 2009 (Monday only, 10–5).

➕ F6 ✉ Via dei Calzaiuoli ☎ 055 284 944
🕐 Daily 10–5 🚌 C1 ♿ Good 🎟 Free

PIAZZA DELLA REPUBBLICA

This grandiose square in the middle of Florence, on the site of the old market, was built in the 1870s, when Florence briefly was the capital of Italy. Florentines are not fond of the square's architecture nor its crass neoclassical triumphal arch, but it is an unusually large open space, where you can breathe a little and let a child run off some energy. All around are excellent grand cafés, if somewhat overpriced.

➕ F6 🚌 C2 ♿ Good

PONTE SANTA TRINITÀ

The finest of Florence's bridges dates back to 1252, although what you see today is a well-executed replica of Ammannati's bridge built in 1567 and destroyed by the Nazis in 1944. Ammannati was commissioned by Cosimo I and probably consulted Michelangelo in his designs. Lovely views of Florence, especially the Ponte Vecchio, are to be had from here.

➕ E6 🚌 C3, D ♿ Good 🎟 Free

SAN MARTINO DEL VESCOVO

This tiny oratory is set right in the heart of medieval Florence. Don't miss the *lunette* frescoes on the upper walls.

➕ F6 ✉ Piazza San Martino, Via Dante Alighieri 🕐 Mon–Sat 10–12, 3–5 (closed Fri pm) 🚌 C2 ♿ Acceptable 🎟 Free

The city's guild workers depicted on the wall of the Orsanmichele

Summer, *one of the 'Seasons' statues on the Ponte Santa Trinità*

Dante's Florence

A short walk through the district where Dante lived, worked and played, and then on to the eastern part of the city to Sante Croce.

DISTANCE: 1km (0.5 miles) approx **ALLOW:** 1 hour including visits

START

BATTISTERO (▷ 55)
✚ F5 🚌 C1, C2

END

SANTA CROCE (▷ 33)
✚ H6 🚌 C1, C2, C3

1 Start at the Baptistery (▷ 55), where the poet Dante Alighieri was baptized. At that time, it was not covered with the marble facing that adorns the facade today.

8 Dante's sarcophagus, inside the church, is empty. Despite all his connections with the city of Florence, Dante was buried in Ravenna.

2 According to tradition Dante watched the construction of the cathedral from the Sasso di Dante, a stone (marked) in the wall between Via dello Studio and Via del Proconsolo, opposite the Duomo.

7 Take the second left, Via dell'Anguillara, to reach Piazza Santa Croce. The streets are dotted with artisans' workshops. Outside the church of Santa Croce (▷ 33) there is a 19th-century statue of Dante.

3 Take Via dello Studio. Turn left at Via del Corso and take the first right onto Via di Santa Margherita. This leads to the Casa di Dante (▷ 37), one-time home of the author.

Dante often saw Beatrice here and the Badia's bell would have punctuated Dante's daily life. Exit and turn onto Via del Proconsolo, past the Bargello (▷ 24–25), which was being built in Dante's time.

Opposite is San Martino del Vescovo (▷ 39), where Dante's family worshipped. Back toward Via del Corso is Santa Margherita, where his Beatrice went to Mass.

5 From Santa Margherita turn left onto Via Dante Alighieri for the entrance of the Badia (▷ 37).

WALK

THE SOUTH CENTRO

ANGELA CAPUTI

www.angelacaputi.com
Angela Caputi is the place to look for bright, bold and highly original costume jewellery. Clothing and accessories to go with the pendant or earrings you have just bought are also stocked.
🞤 F6 ✉ Borgo Santi Apostoli 44–46r ☎ 055 292 993 🚍 C3, D

A. RISALITI

www.a-risaliti.com
'Risaliti' means a golden guarantee, and that's what you get at this jewellers that oozes class. Distinguished clients, including Bette Davis and Ava Gardner, have admired their beautiful handcrafted pieces; gold with precious stones in both classic and modern designs.
🞤 F6 ✉ Ponte Vecchio 27–29r ☎ 055 294 656 🚍 C3, D

ARMANDO POGGI

www.apoggi.com
One of the widest selections of porcelain in the city. Stocks Guiseppi Armani figurines and Richard Ginori porcelain.
🞤 F5 ✉ Via Calzaiuoli 103r and 116r ☎ 055 211 719 🚍 C2

ARTE DEL CIOCCOLATO

www.artedelcioccolato.it
Chocolatier par excellence Roberto Catinari learned his craft in Switzerland before returning to his native Tuscany. His shop is a shrine to the best in chocolate-making—first-class ingredients, superb recipes and delicious results.
🞤 E6 ✉ Via Porta Rossi (corner with Via de' Tornabuoni) ☎ 055 217 136 🚍 C3, D

BACCANI

A beautiful shop, established in 1903. The old interior is filled with prints, engravings, paintings and old maps. Prices vary from very reasonable to very expensive.
🞤 D5 ✉ Borgo Ognissanti 22r ☎ 055 214 467 🚍 C3

IL BISONTE

www.ilbisonte.com
With everything stamped with the trademark bison, this brand is at the cutting

GOLD FACTS

A dazzling array of gold is for sale all over Florence, most notably on the Ponte Vecchio: In 1593 Ferdinand I decreed that only goldsmiths and jewellers should work there and it has remained that way ever since. The gold sold in Florence is 18 carat, often expressed as a rather confusing 750 per cent (with the per cent sign actually referring to 1,000). Gold is also found—at somewhat lower prices—in the Santa Croce area, where, in accordance with tradition, all gold jewellery and other items are sold by weight.

edge of leather bags and accessories.
🞤 E6 ✉ Via del Parione 31r ☎ 055 215 772 🚍 C3

LA BOTTEGA DELLA FRUTTA

The owners search high and low for more unusual products for this family-run business. The select produce includes fresh fruit, cheese, yogurts, pasta, balsamic vinegar and wine.
🞤 E5 ✉ Via dei Federighi 31r ☎ 055 239 8590 🚍 C3

CASSETTI

www.cassetti.it
Maria Grazia's collection of quality jewellery, including period items, has attracted attention from famous people such as David Bowie, Bill Clinton and Liz Taylor.
🞤 F6 ✉ Ponte Vecchio 33–52–54r ☎ 055 239 6028 🚍 C3, D

CELLERINI

www.cellerini.it
Elegant and sophisticated leather bags of outstanding quality. Styles tend to be wonderfully simple yet cleverly designed. Popular among fashionistas.
🞤 E5 ✉ Via del Sole 37r ☎ 055 282 533 🚍 C2, C3, D

COIN

www.coin.it
A huge clothing and design emporium with a vast range of goods at reasonable prices on the Via dei Calzaiuoli. Open on Sunday.

F5 ✉ Via dei Calzaiuoli 56r ☎ 055 280 531 🚌 C2

DUCCI
www.duccishop.com
There is a huge selection of tinted lithographs and prints here, framed and unframed. Some of the unusual objets d'art include wood carvings.
E6 ✉ Lungarno Corsini 24r ☎ 055 214 550 🚌 C3, D

EMILIO CAVALLINI
www.emiliocavallini.com
A wacky collection of socks and hosiery.
E6 ✉ Via della Vigna Nuova 24r ☎ 055 238 2789 🚌 C3

EMILIO PUCCI
www.emiliopucci.com
A renowned Florentine fashion house created in 1950 by Marquis Emilio Pucci. This store on Via de' Tornabuoni sells fantastic, very pricey separates, silk shirts, shoes and accessories.
E6 ✉ Via de' Tornabuoni 20–22r ☎ 055 265 8082 🚌 C3

FARMACIA MOLTENI
www.farmacia-molteni.com
This historic pharmacy, one of the oldest in Florence, is open 24 hours a day. It is worth a visit to view the beautiful interior alone, but in addition it has a good range of cosmetics and natural products.
F5 ✉ Via dei Calzaiuoli 7r ☎ 055 215 472 🚌 C2

FRATELLI PICCINI
www.fratellipiccini.com
If you go jewellery shopping on the Ponte Vecchio, make sure you take in Piccini's. They have lovely gold charms, which make a nice gift.
F6 ✉ Ponte Vecchio 23r ☎ 055 294 768 🚌 C3, D

FRATELLI ROSSETTI
www.fratellirossetti.com
Beautifully crafted shoes and boots in classic Italian styles for men and women.
F5 ✉ Piazza della Repubblica 43–45r ☎ 055 216 656 🚌 C2

STYLISH CITY
One of Florence's many claims to fame is as the headquarters of Gucci. It was also in Florence, in 1927, that Salvatore Ferragamo established himself, after having made his reputation in Hollywood crafting shoes for the likes of Greta Garbo, Vivien Leigh, Gloria Swanson and the gladiators in Cecil B. de Mille costume epics. This family still administers a fashion empire, producing accessories and clothes as well as the trademark shoes. Ties are also for sale in Florence at remarkably good prices. The market of San Lorenzo is the least expensive place, but even on the Ponte Vecchio the prices are agreeable!

FURLA
www.furla.com
Chic, handsomely designed leather bags and belts at prices that are less astronomic than elsewhere. There is another branch of the store at Via della Vigna Nuova 47.
F5 ✉ Via dei Calzaiuoli 47r ☎ 055 238 2883 🚌 C2

THE GOLD CORNER
This frequent tour-group stop in Piazza Sante Croce sells gold by weight along with typical Italian cameos and coral.
G6 ✉ Piazza Santa Croce 15r ☎ 055 241 971 🚌 C1, C2, C3

GUCCI
A predictably elegant and pricey shop; headquarters of the Gucci empire.
E6 ✉ Via de' Tornabuoni 73r ☎ 055 264 011 🚌 C3

LEATHER SCHOOL OF SANTA CROCE
www.scuoladelcuoio.com
At the back of Santa Croce church, off Via di San Giuseppe, this workshop sells quality craftsmanship at the on-site shop.
G6 ✉ Via San Guiseppe 5r (off Piazza Santa Croce) ☎ 055 244 533 🚌 C1, C2, C3

LETIZIA FIORINI
This beautiful little shop is also the artist's workshop, where she makes charming, and not expensive, handcrafted puppets, dolls and other toys. It's hard to

resist buying a Pinocchio puppet or a jack-in-the-box to take home.

⊞ E6 ✉ Via del Parione 60r ☎ 055 216 504 ▣ C3

LUISA VIA ROMA
www.luisaviaroma.com
A popular spot for Florence's image-conscious men and women. Eye-catching window displays conceal a sleek interior over two floors where well-known labels rub shoulders with Luisa's own designs.

⊞ F5 ✉ Via Roma 19–21r ☎ 055 906 4116 ▣ C2

MARTELLI
www.martelligloves.it
This Florence institution has manufactured hand-made gloves since 1967 and sells an amazing selection, in every hue and fabric imaginable.

⊞ F6 ✉ Via Por Santa Maria 18r ☎ 055 239 6395 ▣ C3, D

MAX & CO
The trendy branch of MaxMara sells well-designed high-fashion pieces to a mainly teen-age clientele, plus a range of classics with a contemporary twist.

⊞ F5 ✉ Via dei Calzaiuoli 89r ☎ 055 288 656 ▣ C2

MISURI
This is one of the best leather factories in the Santa Croce area.

⊞ G6 ✉ Piazza Santa Croce 20r ☎ 055 240 995 ▣ C1, C2, C3

OLFATTORIO
www.olfattorio.it
Even if you don't want to buy, take a look at the striking display and interior of this perfumery. Let an expert find the fragrance to suit you, most of which are hand-made in France or the UK. There is also a quirky little museum dedicated to early 20th-century powder boxes.

⊞ E6 ✉ Via de' Tornabuoni 6 ☎ 055 286 925 ▣ C3

PAMPALONI
www.pampaloni.com
As well as ceramics, this high-quality gift shop aimed at the wedding-present market has a range of silverware and porcelain.

⊞ F6 ✉ Borgo Santi Apostoli 47r ☎ 055 289 094 ▣ C3, D

WHAT'S AN ANTIQUE

Under Italian law an antique need not be old, but need only be made of old materials. For this reason, what would be called reproduction elsewhere is called an antique in Italy. Many shops in Florence sell antiques, from the glamorous international emporia on Borgo Ognissanti to the flea market in Piazza dei Ciompi—there are whole streets of them. The most important include Borgo Ognissanti and Via Maggio, for very expensive antiques finely displayed.

PARENTI
Even those who say they don't like jewellery end up swooning over Parenti's eclectic mix of styles and shapes, rang-ing from art nouveau to sheer 1970s glitz.

⊞ E6 ✉ Via de' Tornabuoni 93r ☎ 055 214 438 ▣ C3

PARIONE
www.parione.it
This prestigious chain of stationers selling hand-decorated marbled paper, personalized sta-tionery and accessories also has a collection of beautifully crafted music boxes and miniatures.

⊞ E6 ✉ Via Parione 10r ☎ 055 215 684 ▣ C3

PEGNA
www.pegna.it
This lovely old-fashioned shop, around since 1860, sells its delicious foods supermarket-style. Buy fine cheeses, olive oils, cakes, wines, salamis, chocolates and lots more.

⊞ F5 ✉ Via dello Studio 8 ☎ 055 282 701/2 ▣ C2

PER BACCO
A welcome addition to the city, this *enoteca* con-ceals in its vaults more than 500 different Italian wines, with pride of place going to those produced locally. They prefer small firms for their attention to detail and eco-friendly production methods.

⊞ F6 ✉ Borgo SS. Apostoli 21/23r ☎ 055 292 646 ▣ C3, D

PINEIDER

www.pineider.com

A chic and expensive stationery and book-binding business that was founded in 1774. One of the characteristic papers covering diaries and address books is decorated with great artists' signatures.

➕ F6 ✉ Piazza della Signoria 13–14r ☎ 055 284 655 🚌 C1, C2

PRADA–DONNA

www.prada.com

The world's most popular Italian fashion house of the moment. The headquarters are in Milan but there's a good range of women's clothes, shoes, bags and accessories in this branch.

➕ E6 ✉ Via de' Tornabuoni 53r ☎ 055 267 471 🚌 C2

LA RINASCENTE

www.rinascente.it

This classy department store is where smart Florentines shop. It drips designer labels, although prices are good and there's the odd find to be made. There are also perfumery, lingerie and other departments for those who like to shop for everything under one roof.

➕ F5 ✉ Piazza della Repubblica 1 ☎ 055 219 113 🚌 C2

ROBERTO CAVALLI

www.robertocavalli.com

One of Tuscany's most renowned designers, known for his flamboyant styles using fur and wild prints. Relax at the café.

➕ E6 ✉ Via de' Tornabuoni 83r ☎ 055 239 6226 🚌 C2

ROMANO

www.romanofirenze.com

For a huge variety of shoes, boots and sandals for both men and women, Romano has perhaps the most comprehensive selection in the city. You'll see trendy young Florentines trying on kitten heels next to older women looking at more conservative, traditional styles. Not too pricey.

➕ F5 ✉ Via Speziali 10r ☎ 055 216 535 🚌 C1

SALVATORE FERRAGAMO

www.salvatoreferragamo.it

Designer shoes in the Palazzo Spini Feroni, which has a museum of shoes (▷ 38). Considered to be

the leading brand in Italian shoes and bags.

➕ E6 ✉ Via de' Tornabuoni 4r–14r ☎ 055 292 123 🚌 C2

SISLEY

Italian Sisleys have a much wider selection of fashion than their British counterparts, and the prices are up to 30 per cent lower, too. The Benetton subsidiary has a wide range of separates and accessories, as well as a number of the season's unmissable buys.

➕ F5 ✉ Via Roma 11–13r ☎ 055 286 669 🚌 C1

VALMAR

www.valmar-florence.com

A compact shop that sells trims and finishings for fashion and upholstery.

➕ F6 ✉ Via Porta Rossa 53r ☎ 055 284 493 🚌 C1, C2, C3

VANDA NENCIONI

Pretty gilded frames, as well as period and modern prints.

➕ F6 ✉ Via della Condotta 25r ☎ 055 215 345 🚌 C1

VINARIUS

www.vinarius.net

Sample a glass before you buy at this elegant *enoteca*; experts will help you make your selection. Also local extra virgin olive oil, balsamic vinegar and delicacies made with truffles and honey.

➕ G6 ✉ Borgo Santa Croce 15r ☎ 055 200 1216 🚌 C1, C2, C3

CLOTHES SHOPPING

The most exclusive designers are in the district of Via de' Tornabuoni and Via della Vigna Nuova. The area around Piazza della Repubblica and Via dei Calzaiuoli has a good range of major high-street clothes shops, such as MaxMara. In the streets east of Via dei Calzaiuoli there are many mid-range fashion boutiques. The areas around Santa Croce and San Lorenzo sell bargain fashions to the tourist market.

Entertainment and Nightlife

CHIESA DE' SANTA MARIA DE RICCI

During the free concerts held at 9.15 most nights, you can sample the distinctive sound of Florentine organ music in a wonderfully evocative setting. Check for days.

F5 ☒ Via del Corso ☎ 055 289 367 ⬛ C2

HARRY'S BAR

www.harrysbarfirenze.it
This American bar, on the banks of the Arno, is one of the best places in the city for cocktails. The international food is also good.

D6 ☒ Lungarno Vespucci 22r ☎ 055 239 6700 ⬛ C3, D

LOONEES

This central, friendly, studenty basement bar is popular with tourists and has occasional live music playing mainly British and American classic covers.

F6 ☒ Via Porta Rossa 15 ☎ 338 875 5725 ⬛ C2, C3, D

MAYDAY

Locals swarm around this stylish music bar where, into the early hours, you can enjoy wine, good beer or a cocktail while listening to live music.

F6 ☒ Via Dante Alighieri 16r ☎ 055 238 1290 ⏱ Closed Sun ⬛ C2

ODEON CINEHALL

www.cinehall.it
Housed in the art nouveau Palazzo Strozzino,

the cinema has retained original sculptures, tapestries and a stained-glass cupola. Probably the best place in the city for original sound films in English.

E6 ☒ Piazza Strozzi ☎ 055 214 068 ⏱ Times vary. Check for schedule ⬛ C2

RED GARTER

www.redgarterflorence.com
Established in 1962, this American-style bar attracts students and younger tourists, and remains one of the most popular in the city. There is live music most nights, with cocktails and beers, food and live sports TV, too.

G6 ☒ Via de' Benci 33r ☎ 055 248 0909 ⏱ Daily 5pm–2am ⬛ C1, C3

SLOWLY CAFÈ

www.slowlycafe.com
Chill out to eclectic music at this loft-inspired space. The trendy crowd sips classic cocktails and

EVENING STROLL

Going out in Florence in the evening doesn't have to mean actually going anywhere. In summer a really enjoyable and popular way of spending time after dinner is to stroll through the streets of the historic section, stopping off for an ice cream or a drink at a bar. What's more is that you'll see plenty of groups of Italians of all ages and genders doing exactly the same thing.

aperitifs while nibbling on Tuscan snacks.

F6 ☒ Via Porta Rossa 63r ☎ 055 264 5354 ⏱ Daily 7pm–2am ⬛ C2, C3, D

TEATRO VERDI

www.teatroverdionline.it
The Teatro Verdi, founded in 1854, testifies to the importance of the arts in Florentine life. The theatre puts on drama, ballet and opera from January to April. The excellent Orchestra della Toscana plays here between December and May.

G6 ☒ Via Ghibellina 99 ☎ 055 212 320; 055 210 804 ⬛ 14, 23, C2

TWICE

www.twiceclub.com
Go early for a drink, food or jazz, or wait until late when the pace picks up. You may want to check what's playing in advance. It's always popular, so expect a large crowd.

G6 ☒ Via Giuseppe Verdi 57r ☎ 055 247 356 ⏱ Nightly, bar opens 9pm. Late night schedule varies, check website ⬛ 14, 23, C2

YAB

www.yab.it
One of Florence's most central clubs, this is often full of young visitors. Music and fashions here are up to date. The theatrical surroundings add to the overall atmosphere.

F6 ☒ Via Sassetti 5r ☎ 055 215 160 ⏱ Closed some evenings, call for details. Closed Jun–Sep ⬛ C2

Restaurants

PRICES

Prices are approximate, based on a 3-course meal for one person.

€€€ over €55
€€ €35–€55
€ under €35

ALLE MURATE (€€€)

www.allemurate.it
Sophisticated restaurant where traditional Tuscan cooking is given an innovative twist. Try *tagliatelle all'olio nuovo, tonne fresco e timo* (noodles with freshly pressed olive oil, tuna and thyme). The soft lighting and candles make for an intimate dining experience.
🚹 G6 ⊠ Via del Proconsolo 16r ☎ 055 240 618 🌐 Closed Mon 🚌 C2

ANTICO BARILE (€€)

www.anticobarile.com
Enjoy good Tuscan and international cuisine in the heart of city, close to Piazza della Repubblica and the Duomo. The elegantly rustic setting has some interesting features and a mezzanine floor. Helpful service and competitive prices.
🚹 F6 ⊠ Via dei Cerchi 40r ☎ 055 213 142 🚌 C2

BALDOVINO (€€)

www.baldovino.com
This bustling trattoria not far from Piazza Santa Croce serves great pizza, cooked in a wood-burning oven, in a relaxed ambience. Great for kids.

The wide-ranging menu is constantly changing.
🚹 H6 ⊠ Via San Giuseppe 22r ☎ 055 241 773 🚌 C1, C2, C3

BELLE DONNE (€–€€)

www.casatrattoria.com
An inexpensive option in an expensive part of town. It's small, modest and you can barely see inside because of the potted plants. The menu has some interestingly prepared vegetables. You will probably share a table with others.
🚹 E5 ⊠ Via delle Belle Donne 16r ☎ 055 238 2609 🚌 C2, D

BOCCADAMA (€€)

www.boccadama.com
Interesting food and good wine, plus views of the Basilica Santa Croce make

this lively historic *enoteca*, which doubles as a restaurant, popular. You can eat on the delightful terrace, and enjoy dishes cooked with top-quality local ingredients.
🚹 G6 ⊠ Piazza Santa Croce 25–26r ☎ 055 243 640 🌐 Closed Tue dinner 🚌 C1, C2, C3

LA BUSSOLA (€€)

www.labussolafirenze.it
La Bussola serves some of the best pizza in town cooked in a traditional wood-burning oven; also good seafood dishes. In a rustic setting with relaxed friendly service where you can eat from the bar.
🚹 F6 ⊠ Via Porta Rossa 58r ☎ 055 293 376 🚌 C2, C3, D

CAFFÈ AMERINI (€€)

The Amerini lies in the main fashionable shopping area, and makes a good venue for taking a break during the day. Be warned though—it gets very popular in the early afternoon. Snacks and a variety of pastries packed with tasty fillings.
🚹 E6 ⊠ Via della Vigna Nuova 63r ☎ 055 284 941 🌐 Closed Sun 🚌 C2

CANTINETTA DEI VERRAZZANO (€€)

www.verrazzano.com
A wonderful wine bar-cum-shop selling breads baked on the premises and wines from the Castello di Verrazzano estates near Greve. Don't

miss the *focaccia* (flat loaf), baked in the wood-burning ovens.

➕ F6 ✉ Via de' Tavolini 18–20r ☎ 055 268 590 🕐 Closed Sun 🚌 C2

IL CIBREO (€€€)

www.edizioniteatrodelsale cibreofirenze.it
This restaurant, one of the city's gastronomic shrines, offers no pasta, but an intriguing range of robust Florentine dishes.

➕ H6 ✉ Via Andea del Verrocchio 8r ☎ 055 244 966 🕐 Closed Sun, Mon and Aug 🚌 C2

COCO LEZZONE (€€€)

Popular with Florentines, with informal white-tiled rooms. The short menu offers Tuscan classics.

➕ E6 ✉ Via del Parioncino 26r ☎ 055 287 178 🕐 Closed Tue dinner and Sun 🚌 C3

DA BENVENUTO (€)

www.trattoriadabenvenuto.it
There's lots of solid Tuscan food to choose from at this long-standing venue in the Santa Croce quarter.

➕ G6 ✉ Via della Mosca 16r ☎ 055 214 833 🚌 C1, C2, C3

LA DECIMA MUSA (€€)

www.ladecimamusa.it
The refined and intimate atmosphere is largely thanks to its diminutive size and wood-panelled walls. La Decima's patron Daniele Bertucci oversees a traditional but refined

Tuscan menu and a first-class wine cellar.

➕ E6 ✉ Via del Parione 50r ☎ 055 294 122 🕐 Closed Sun 🚌 C3

DEI FRESCOBALDI RISTORANTE & WINE BAR (€€)

www.deifrescobaldi.it
On the corner of Piazza della Signoria, Frescobaldi offers traditional Tuscan cuisine, or the chance to eat salads, cheeses and salamis tapas-style in the adjacent wine bar. In the main restaurant choose from pasta dishes or substantial grilled meats. Excellent wine list.

➕ F6 ✉ Via de' Magazzini 2–4r ☎ 055 284 724 🕐 Closed Sun, Mon lunch 🚌 C3

EITO (€€–€€€)

www.eito.it
This corner of Japan in Florence is where

BREAD

Almost all bread in Tuscany is made without salt. This takes some getting used to, but the blandness makes a good background to highly seasoned foods such as the Florentine salami Finocchiona, which is scented with fennel and garlic. And the bread's texture—firm, almost coarse, and very substantial—is wonderful. Strict laws govern what goes into Italian bread: It is free of chemical preservatives.

---

beautifully presented, refined Japanese cooking successfully attempts to arouse new sensations. The delightful ambience of this small restaurant creates a relaxing and intimate atmosphere.

➕ G6 ✉ Via dei Neri 72r ☎ 055 210 940 🕐 Dinner 7–11.30; closed Mon 🚌 C1, C3

ENOTECA PINCHIORRI (€€€)

www.enotecapinchiorri.it
The city's most fashionable and priciest eatery is somewhat serious. For wine connoisseurs it is a must, possessing one of Europe's very finest wine cellars. Reserve ahead.

➕ G6 ✉ Via Ghibellina 87 ☎ 055 242 777/757 🕐 Closed Sun–Wed lunch 🚌 C1, C2, C3

GILLI (€€)

www.gilli.it
A chic, opulent café on the corner of the Piazza della Repubblica; the pastries are renowned (but pricey). Sit outside and indulge in, say, a lavish ice-cream sundae.

➕ F5 ✉ Via Roma 1r ☎ 055 213 896 🕐 Closed Tue 🚌 C2

GIUBBE ROSSE (€€)

www.giubberosse.it
Once the haunt of futurists and the Florentine *avanguardia* scene. The red-jacketed waiters and stylish interiors hint at this illustrious past. Drink coffee and

watch the world go by on the elegant piazza.

✚ F5 ✉ Piazza della Repubblica 13–14r ☎ 055 212 280 🚊 C2

GUSTO LEO (€–€€)

www.gustoleo.com
A good pitstop for lunch at the heart of the city, which attracts many young Italians to its excellent salads, pizza and soup.
✚ G6 ✉ Via del Pronconsolo 8–10r ☎ 055 285 217 🚊 C1, C2

HOSTARIA BIBENDUM (€€€)

www.hbf.royaldemeure.com
In the Hotel Helvetia & Bristol (▷ 112), this restaurant and cocktail bar exudes exclusivity. Expect gilt, chandeliers, draperies and a formal atmosphere. Safe but expertly prepared menu.
✚ E5 ✉ Via dei Pescioni 8r ☎ 055 266 5620 🚊 C2

KOME (€€)

www.komefirenze.it
A trendy sushi and BBQ restaurant in a historic palazzo between stone walls under a gold leaf ceiling. High stools stand alongside a winding counter. Eat hot from the kitchen or choose from the tempting sushi train.
✚ G6 ✉ Via de Benci 41r ☎ 055 200 8009 🕐 Closed Sun 🚊 C1, C3

IL LATINI (€€)

www.illatini.com
Boisterous restaurant offering Tuscan classics

such as *pappardelle con la lepre* (wide strips of pasta with hare sauce). Other interesting dishes include wild boar *dolce-forte* (wild boar stewed in honey, dried fuit and pine-nut sauce). Seating is at communal tables.
✚ E5 ✉ Via dei Palchetti 6r ☎ 055 210 916 🕐 Closed Mon 🚊 C1, C3

OLIVIERO (€€€)

www.ristorante-oliviero.it
Excellent service, soft fabric-filled interiors and superb Tuscan food are the main characteristics of this eatery. Wild boar, guinea fowl and rabbit all feature on the menu. Sublime soups, exquisite vegetables and innovative pasta creations.
✚ E6 ✉ Via delle Terme 51r ☎ 055 287 643 🕐 Dinner only; closed Sun 🚊 C2

PIZZA AT ITS BEST

As in every Italian town, pizzas are all over and many shops sell *pizza a taglio* (cut pizza). A good option for a quick snack is a slice. In addition to the standard margherita pizza (tomato and mozzarella), you will find all kinds of other delicious toppings, such as courgette (zucchini) flowers and aubergine (eggplant). Go when they're busy and the turnover is high to avoid eating cold pizza that's been sitting around for a while.

ORVM (€€€)

Dine in style in an elegant art deco setting at the Westin Excelsior Hotel, with views of the River Arno. Here you will find contemporary Mediterranean cuisine and Tuscan influences that promote healthy cooking using the finest seasonal ingredients.
✚ D5 ✉ Piazza Ognissanti 3 ☎ 055 271 151 🚊 C3

OSTERIA DE' BENCI (€)

www.osteriadeibenci.it
A genuine Florentine *osteria*. Start with *crostini* (Tuscan *bruschetta*— toasted bread served with spreads, cheeses and cold meats) then choose from the day's menu that often includes spaghetti in red wine and/or a delicious vegetable soup. The meat dishes are particularly good.
✚ G6 ✉ Via de' Benci 13r ☎ 055 234 4923 🕐 Closed Aug 🚊 C1, C3

PALLOTTINO (€€)

www.trattoriapallottino.com
In business for around 100 years, this traditional trattoria near Santa Croce has small dining rooms, wooden tables and candles. The frequently changing menu uses what's in season. The pasta dishes are truly excellent.
✚ G6 ✉ Via Isola delle Stinche 1r ☎ 055 289 573 🕐 Closed Mon, Aug 🚊 C1, C3

PASZKOWSKI (€€–€€€)

www.paszkowski.it

On the grandiose Piazza della Repubblica, this is a lovely, if expensive, old-world café and tearoom where a piano bar adds a note of refinement to an already delightful interior.

🚹 F5 🖂 Piazza della Repubblica 6r ☎ 055 213 896 🚌 C2

PERCHÉ NO! (€)

www.percheno.firenze.it

'Why not!' has to be a good name for an ice-cream place. Founded in 1939, this shop still produces plenty of new tastes to get excited about. It is renowned for its *semifreddi*, which come in creamy tastes such as hazelnut mousse and *zuppa inglese* (trifle).

🚹 F6 🖂 Via dei Tavolini 19r ☎ 055 239 8969 🚌 C2

PROCACCI (€–€€)

www.antinori.it

A delightful bar that is something of a legend because of its *panini tartufati*, sandwiches made with a white truffle puree. Just the thing to accompany a glass of Tuscan wine.

🚹 E5 🖂 Via de' Tornabuoni 64r ☎ 055 211 656 🚌 C2

RIVOIRE (€€–€€€)

www.rivoire.it

This café, opened in the 1870s, is a Florentine institution. At Rivoire, you pay for the view, but it's well worth the money. Set on the Piazza della Signoria, looking out toward the Palazzo Vecchio, this is the ideal place to relax after a hectic visit to the Uffizi.

🚹 F6 🖂 Piazza della Signoria 5r ☎ 055 214 412 🕐 Closed Mon and 2 weeks in Jan 🚌 C1, C3, D

TRATTORIA 13 GOBBI (€€)

www.casatrattoria.com

If you want character and romantic ambience, Gobbi oozes both with its candlelight and warm atmosphere. The traditional Florentine and Tuscan menu has been given a lighter touch and desserts are to die for.

🚹 D5 🖂 Via del Porcellana 9r ☎ 055 284 015 🚌 C2

TRATTORIA MARIONE (€)

www.casatrattoria.com

Good home cooking based on local ingredients. Well-prepared dishes include soup, with classic Tuscan vegetable

STAND OR SIT

You will almost always pay a premium to sit down and to enjoy the privilege of waiter service at coffee shops, cafés and gelaterie that often double up as all-round bars to be enjoyed during the day. If you stand, which is less expensive, you are generally not expected to linger too long after finishing your refreshment.

soup, *ribollito*, on the menu, and tripe.

🚹 E5 🖂 Via della Spada 27r ☎ 055 214 756 🚌 C2

TRATTORIA PONTE VECCHIO (€€–€€€)

www.trattoriapontevecchio.com

A stone's throw from the Ponte Vecchio, this trattoria is inevitably popular with visitors and you cannot fault the Tuscan cuisine. One of the house specials is tagliatelle with porcini mushrooms.

🚹 F6 🖂 Lungarno Archibusieri 8r ☎ 055 292 289 🚌 C3, D

VIVOLI (€)

www.vivoli.it

Vivoli is legendary; the family have been making ice cream since the 1930s. If you don't mind the wait, the rewards are delicious. Lots of choices, including an extra creamy *mousse di amaretto*. All served in *coppette* (different-size cups); Vivoli is a no-cone zone.

🚹 G6 🖂 Via Isola delle Stinche 7r ☎ 055 292 334 🕐 Closed Mon 🚌 C2

WINTER GARDEN BY CAINO (€€€)

The lavish interior of the restaurant at the grand St. Regis Florence hotel (▷ 112) has a striking contemporary feel. The well-balanced menu pays close attention to Tuscan tastes.

🚹 D5 🖂 St. Regis Florence, Piazza Ognissanti 1 ☎ 055 2716 3770 🚌 C3

A district abundant with fine churches, the epitome of which is the magnificent Duomo.

2

3

VIALE FILIPPO STROZZI

Palazzo dei Congressi

Via della Fortezza

Via C Ridolfi

Via Barbano

Bettino Ricasoli

Piazza dell' Indipendenza

Ubaldino Peruzzi

Via F Zanobi

Via delle Ruote

Via S Reparata

Via F Bartolommei

Via Vendette

Via delle Ruote

Ex Convento di S Apollonia

Via Arazzi

4

Palazzo Affari

Via B Cennini

VIA VALFONDA

Via a Fiume

Cenatolo di Foligno

VIA

Via Nazionale

Via Panicale

Via S Antonino

Faenza

GUELFA

Biblioteca Marucelliana

SAN GIOVANNI

VIA CAVOUR

Mercato Centrale

Piazza del Mercato Centrale

Borgo la Noce

Via de' Conti

Via de' Ginori

Via Ricasoli

Palazz. Geri

SANTA MARIA NOVELLA

V S Cat da Siena

VIA LUIGI ALAMANNI

Obelisco dell' Unità d'Italia

VIA DELLA SCALA

Via degli Alberi

Via del Melarancio

Santa Maria Novella

Piazza dell' Unità Italiana

Cappelle Medicee

San Lorenzo

Biblioteca Laurenziana

Canto de' Nelli

Mercato San Lorenzo

Borgo S Lorenzo

VIA DE' MARTELLI

Teatro Reg Toscano

Teatro Niccolini

Palazz. Pucci

Palazzo Medici-Riccardi

Museo dell'Opera del Duomo

Palazzuolo

Via del Giglio

VIA PANZANI

Via de' Banchi

Piazza Santa Maria Novella

VIA DE' CERRETANI

Battistero

Piazza d S Giovanni

Duomo

Piazza del Duomo

5

VIA D RONDINELLI

Via degli Agli

Via de' Pecori

Campanile

Via d' Oche

Via di

Via de' Roma

6

7

0   250 m

0   250 yds

D   **E**   **F**

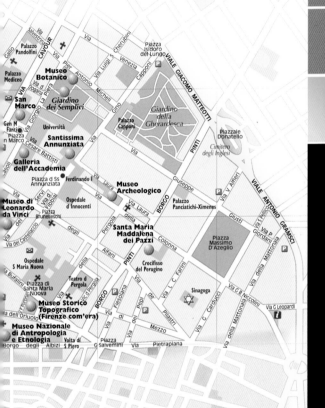

G   H   J

Bronze panel from Ghiberti's 'Gates of Paradise' (right) on the Battistero (left)

Battistero

Perhaps the most loved of all Florence's edifices is the beautiful octagonal Baptistery referred to by Dante as his 'bel San Giovanni', and dedicated to St. John the Baptist, the city's patron saint.

Roman origins The Baptistery is one of the oldest buildings in the city: Remains of a Roman palace lie under it, and the dates given for the present construction vary between the fifth and the seventh centuries AD. For many centuries it was the place where Florentines were baptized and it is clear where the font stood until its removal in 1576.

Rich ornament The entire outer surface is covered with a beautiful design of white and green marble, added between the 11th and 13th centuries. Inside, the ceiling is encrusted with stunning mosaics: Above the altar, designs show the Virgin and St. John the Baptist; the main design depicts the *Last Judgement*, with the sinful being devoured by diabolical creatures, while the virtuous ascend to heaven. Do not miss the tessellated floor, almost Islamic in its intricate geometry.

Bronze doors The Baptistery is renowned, above all, for its bronze doors: the south doors, by Pisano (1336), and Ghiberti's north and east doors (1403–24 and 1425–52). The east doors, referred to by Michelangelo as the 'Gates of Paradise', are divided into 10 panels depicting Old Testament scenes. In 1990 copies of these doors replaced the originals, which are on view in the Museo dell'Opera del Duomo (▷ 62).

THE BASICS

www.operaduomo.firenze.it
✚ F5
✉ Piazza San Giovanni
☎ 055 230 2885
🕐 Apr–Sep Mon–Wed 11.15–7, Thu–Sat 8.30am–11pm, Sun and 1st Sat of month 8.30–2; Oct–Mar Mon–Sat 11.15–7, Sun and 1st Sat of month 8.30–2 (last entrance 30 min before closing).
🚌 C1, C2
♿ Good
💶 Moderate; joint ticket with Duomo and Campanile expensive

HIGHLIGHTS

● 13th-century mosaics of the *Last Judgement*
● Ghiberti's east doors
● Pisano's south doors
● Zodiac pavement
● Romanesque marble exterior

Campanile

The superb bell tower affords fantastic views of the city—the climb is worth the effort

THE BASICS

➕ F5
✉ Piazza del Duomo
☎ 055 230 2885
🕐 Daily 8.30–7.30 (last admission 40 min before closing)
🚌 C1, C2
♿ Non-existent; no elevator, 414 steps
💰 Expensive

HIGHLIGHTS

● Views from the top
● Reliefs by Pisano and della Robbia

Tall and beautifully proportioned, the bell tower of the Duomo is one of the loveliest in Italy and adds a calm and graceful note to the otherwise busy cathedral complex.

Multiple effort The Campanile, or bell tower, of the Duomo rises to 85m (279ft). It was begun in 1334 and completed in 1359. Giotto was involved in its design, but by the time of his death in 1337 only the base had been completed. Andrea Pisano completed the second floor and the tower was finished by Francesco Talenti.

Relief sculpture The outer surface is decorated in the same polychrome marble as the Duomo: white marble from Carrara, green marble from Prato and pink marble from the Maremma. Around the bottom are two sets of relief sculptures: The lower tier is in hexagonal panels, the upper tier in diamonds. What you see are in fact copies; the originals have been moved to the Museo dell'Opera del Duomo (▷ 62) to prevent further atmospheric damage. The reliefs in the hexagonal panels, which were executed by Pisano (although some are believed to have been designed by Giotto), show the Creation of Man, the Arts and the Industries. On the north face are the five Liberal Arts (grammar, philosophy, music, arithmetic and astrology), executed by Luca della Robbia. The upper tier of reliefs, also the work of Pisano, illustrates the Seven Planets, the Seven Virtues and the Liberal Arts; the Seven Sacraments are attributed to Alberto Arnoldi.

Maddona and Child *by Michaelangelo (left); the Medici Chapels (right)*

Cappelle Medicee

Of all the places in Florence associated with Michelangelo, the Medici Chapels, the mausoleum of the Medici family, are the most intriguing: with tomb sculptures, *Madonna and Child*, and sketches.

Burial places The mausoleum of the Medici family is in three distinct parts of the church of San Lorenzo (▷ 64): the crypt, the Cappella dei Principi and the Sagrestia Nuova. The crypt was where the bodies of minor members of the dynasty were unceremoniously dumped. Tidied up in the 19th century, it now houses tomb slabs. In the Cappella dei Principi is a huge dome by Bernado Buontalenti, begun in 1604 and not completed until the 20th century. The inner surface is decorated in a heavy, grandiose way that speaks of political tyranny: The Medici coat of arms is rarely out of view. The tombs of six Medici Grand Dukes are in the chapel beneath the dome.

New Sacristy Right of the altar, the Sagrestia Nuova, built by Michelangelo between 1520 and 1534, is a reminder that the Medici were enlightened patrons. Michelangelo sculpted figures representing *Night and Day*, and *Dawn and Dusk* to adorn the tombs of Lorenzo, Duke of Urbino (1492–1519), and Giuliano, Duke of Nemours (1479–1516). The figure of *Night*, with moon, owl and mask, is one of his finest works. The *Madonna and Child* (1521) is by Michelangelo as well. In a room left of the altar are some superb charcoal drawings found in 1975 and attributed to Michelangelo.

THE BASICS

www.polomuseale.firenze.it

➕ F5

✉ Piazza Madonna degli Aldobrandini 6

☎ 055 294 833

🕐 Daily 8.15–1.50 (last admission 30 min before closing); closed 1st, 3rd, 5th Mon, 2nd, 4th Sun of month and 1 Jan, 1 May, 25 Dec

🚌 C1, C2

♿ Poor; ask for assistance

💷 Expensive

❓ English audio guides (moderate)

HIGHLIGHTS

● Michelangelo's *Night*
● The figure of Lorenzo, Duke of Urbino
● Michelangelo's *Madonna and Child*
● Sketches attributed to Michelangelo
● Charcoal drawings by Michelangelo

Duomo

HIGHLIGHTS

● Brunelleschi's dome
● Santa Reparata remains
● Uccello's mural to a 14th-century Captain-General

TIP

● You will not be allowed into the Duomo wearing a sleeveless top or skimpy shorts.

The famous dome of this cathedral dominates the Florence skyline, with its eight white ribs on a background of terracotta tiles. From close up, the size of the building is overwhelming.

Long-term build The cathedral of Santa Maria del Fiori, the Florence Duomo, is a vast Gothic structure built on the site of the seventh-century church of Santa Reparata, whose remains can be seen in the crypt. It was built at the end of the 13th century, although the colossal dome, which dominates the exterior, was not added until the 15th century, and the facade was not finished until the 19th century. The exterior is a decorative riot of pink, white and green marble; the interior is stark and plain. The clock above the entrance on the west wall inside was designed in 1443 by Paolo

Clockwise from left: Crowds gather beneath the Duomo; the cupola is crowned by a lantern; intricate detail enhances the cathedral; Dante and his Worlds *by Domenico di Michelino (1465); mosaic above the Duomo's main door; Vasari's frescoes of* The Last Judgement*; viewed from a height, the cupola is the glory of the Duomo*

Uccello in line with the *ora italica*, according to which the 24th hour of the day ends at sunset.

Roman influences Built by Filippo Brunelleschi, who won the competition for its commission in 1418, the dome is egg-shaped and was made without scaffolding. Its herringbone brickwork was copied from the Pantheon in Rome. The best way to see the dome is to climb its 463 steps. The route takes you through the interior, where you can see Vasari's much-reviled frescoes of *The Last Judgement* (1572–79), and toward the lantern, from which the views are fantastic.

Explosion At Easter the *Scoppio del Carro*, a Mass-cum-theatrical pageant, ends with a mechanical dove being launched from the altar along a wire to the entrance, igniting a cart of fireworks.

THE BASICS

www.operaduomo.firenze.it

✚ F5

✉ Piazza del Duomo

☎ 055 230 2885

🕐 Cathedral Mon–Wed, Fri 10–5; Thu May and Oct 10–4, Jul–Sep 10–5, Nov–Apr 10–4.30; Sat 10–4.45, Sun 1.30–4.45. Dome (access from Porta della Mandoria) Mon–Fri 8.30–7, Sat 8.30–5.40 (last admission 40 min before closing)

🚌 C1, C2

♿ Good (access via Porta di Canonica, south side)

🎟 Free; dome expensive; crypt moderate

Galleria dell'Accademia

HIGHLIGHTS

- Michelangelo's *David*
- Michelangelo's *Prisoners*
- Giambologna's *Rape of the Sabine Women*
- Buonaguida's *Tree of Life*

TIP

- If you want to view *David*, arrive when the museum first opens, or late in the day, to avoid the long lines.

Michelangelo's *David*, exhibited in the Accademia, has a powerful impact: the intensity of his gaze, that assured posture, those huge hands, the anatomical precision of the veins and the muscles.

Art School The Accademia was founded in 1784 to teach techniques of painting, drawing and sculpture. Since 1873 it has housed the world's single most important collection of sculptures by Michelangelo. There are also sculptures by other artists, as well as many paintings, mostly from the Renaissance period.

Masterpiece The main attraction is *David* by Michelangelo, sculpted in 1504 and exhibited outside the Palazzo Vecchio until 1873, when it was transferred to the Accademia to protect it from

St. Francis Receiving the Stigmata *by Taddeo Gaddi, an exhibit in the Galleria dell'Academia (left);* The Tree of Life *or* Jesse's Tree *by Pacino di Buonaguida is preserved in the gallery (middle); the most famous and most visited of all statues in Florence, the magnificent sculpture of* David *by Michelangelo (right)*

environmental damage. It captures the moment at which the young David contemplates defying the giant Goliath. After controversial restoration techniques, David was unveiled in June 2004.

Freedom from stone The *Prisoners* (1505) were made for the tomb of Pope Julius II. The title refers to Michelangelo's belief that when he sculpted a statue, he was freeing the figure from the marble, and the style, particularly preferred by Michelangelo, was called the *non finito* (unfinished). After his death, the *Prisoners* were moved to the Grotta Grande in the Boboli Gardens (▷ 82), where the originals were replaced with casts in 1908. Also seek out the original plaster model for *The Rape of the Sabine Women* (1583), Giambologna's last work; the marble version is in the Loggia dei Lanzi in Piazza della Signoria (▷ 32).

THE BASICS

www.polomuseale.firenze.it
🔒 G4
✉ Via Ricasoli 58–60
☎ 055 294 883
🕐 Tue–Sun 8.15–6.50
(last admission 30 min
before closing); closed
1 May
🚌 C1, C2
♿ Good
💶 Expensive

Museo dell'Opera del Duomo

Detail of a dancing choir by Lucca della Robbia (left); a fresco in the museum (right)

THE BASICS

www.operaduomo.firenze.it
⊞ G5
✉ Piazza del Duomo 9
☎ 055 230 2885
🕐 Daily 9–7.30 (Sun until 1.45)
🚌 C1, C2
♿ Good
💰 Expensive

HIGHLIGHTS

● Singing galleries
● Original panels from the Campanile
● Michelangelo's *Pietà*
● Original panels from the 'Gates of Paradise'
● Donatello's *Maddalena*

There is something very pleasing about the idea of visiting the Cathedral Workshop, the maintenance section of the huge artistic undertaking that the cathedral complex represents.

Refuge from pollution This workshop-museum was founded when the Duomo was built, to maintain the art of the cathedral. Its location was chosen in the 15th century, and it was in its courtyard that Michelangelo sculpted his *David*. Since 1891 it has housed works from the cathedral complex, leaving the Duomo rather empty of art. It is also a refuge for outdoor sculptures.

Michelangelo's *Pietà* On the first level you can see eight of the original ten bronze panels from the east door of the Bapistery by Lorenzo Ghiberti. On the main landing is the *Pietà* (begun c.1550) by Michelangelo. It is said he intended it for his own tomb; the hooded figure of Nicodemus is often interpreted as a self-portrait. The damage to Christ's left leg and arm is believed to have been inflicted by Michelangelo in frustration at his failing skills.

Artists compared The main room on the first floor contains two *cantorie* (singing galleries) that once stood in the Duomo: one by Luca della Robbia (1431–38), the other by Donatello (1433–39). In the room on the left are panels by Pisano from the Campanile (▶ 56); the next room has the construction materials and instruments used for Brunelleschi's dome, such as pulleys and brick moulds.

Opulence in the
Palazzo Medici-Riccardi
(left); fresco by Luca
Giordano (right)

TOP 25

Palazzo Medici-Riccardi

The Medici family ruled Florence with a combination of tyranny and humanity, and this is reflected in the imposing facade of their huge headquarters, with its fearsome lattice of window bars.

Medici origins The Palazzo Medici-Riccardi, now mostly government offices, was the seat of the Medici family from its completion in 1444 until 1540, when Cosimo I moved the Medici residence to the Palazzo Vecchio and this palace was bought by the Riccardi family.

Setting a trend The palace, designed by Michelozzo, was widely imitated in Florence, for example in the Palazzo Strozzi and the Palazzo Pitti (▷ 84–85). It is characterized by huge slabs of stone, rusticated to give a roughly hewn rural appearance. The courtyard is in a lighter style, with a graceful colonnade and black and white *sgraffito* decoration of medallions, based on the designs of Roman intaglios collected by the Medici and displayed in the Museo degli Argenti (▷ 85).

A regal scene Steps right of the entrance lead to the Cappella dei Magi. This tiny chapel has the dazzling fresco cycle depicting the *Journey of the Magi* (1459–63) that Piero de' Medici commissioned from Gozzoli in memory of the Compagnia dei Magi, a religious organization to which the Medici belonged. Portraits of the Medici are believed to have been incorporated into the cast of characters, while the procession recalls the pageantry of the Compagnia dei Magi.

THE BASICS

www.palazzo-medici.it
🔲 F5
✉ Via Cavour 3
☎ 055 276 0340
🕐 Thu–Tue 9–6
🚌 C1, C2
♿ Entrance on Via Cavour;
Cappella poor
💶 Expensive
❓ Entrance to chapel
limited to eight visitors
every seven minutes

HIGHLIGHTS

● Gozzoli's fresco cycle of the *Journey of the Magi* (1459–63)
● Courtyard

San Lorenzo

TOP 25

The Basilica di San Lorenzo (left); the serene cloisters of San Lorenzo (right)

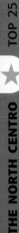

THE NORTH CENTRO   TOP 25

THE BASICS

✚ F5
✉ Piazza San Lorenzo
☎ 055 214 042
🕐 Nov–Feb Mon–Sat 10–5.30; Mar–Oct 1.30–5.30
🚌 C1, C2
♿ Poor
💶 Moderate

HIGHLIGHTS

- Biblioteca Laurenziana (begun 1524)
- Staircase by Michelangelo
- Bronzino's *Martyrdom of St. Lawrence*
- Pulpits by Donatello
- Brunelleschi's Sagrestia Vecchia

San Lorenzo is the parish church and burial place of the Medici and is filled with art commissioned by them. As with the Cappelle Medicee, it is a monument to the family's artistic patronage.

A sacred site San Lorenzo was rebuilt by Filippo Brunelleschi betwen 1425 and 1446, on the site of one of the city's oldest churches (consecrated in AD393). Its rough-hewn ochre exterior was to have been covered with a facade by Michelangelo. This was never added, but a model is in Casa Buonarroti (▷ 37). The most bizarre piece of art here is the statue of Anna Maria Luisa (d.1743), the last of the Medici dynasty, found—like a displaced Limoges porcelain figure—outside of the church. The church, with its *pietra serena* (grey sandstone) columns, is cool and airy. The bronze pulpits (c.1460) depicting the Resurrection and scenes from the life of Christ are Donatello's last work. Bronzino's fresco (facing the altar, left), the *Martyrdom of St. Lawrence* (1569), is an absorbing Mannerist study of the human body in various contortions. Inside Sagrestia Vecchia (Old Sacristy, 1421) are eight *tondi* (circular reliefs) by Donatello depicting the evangelists and scenes from the life of St. John.

Biblioteca Laurenziana The Laurentian Library (tel 055 210 760, www.bml.firenze.sbn.it; Mon–Fri 9.30–1.30) houses the Medici's collection of manuscripts (not on display). This extraordinary example of Mannerist architecture by Michelangelo is left of the church, up a curvaceous *pietra serena* staircase via the cloisters.

The Annuncication
*by Fra Angelico (left);
the ornate exterior
of San Marco (right)*

San Marco

Dominated by the lovely paintings of Fra Angelico, the soothing convent of San Marco has an aura of monastic calm that is conducive to appreciating the religious themes depicted.

Medici motives San Marco was founded in the 13th century by Silvestrine monks. In 1437 Cosimo il Vecchio invited the Dominican monks of Fiesole to move into the convent and had it rebuilt by Michelozzo, a gesture motivated by his guilt for his wealth from banking and by the fact that the Dominicans were useful allies. Ironically, Savonarola, who denounced the decadence of the Medici at the end of the 15th century, came to prominence as the Dominican prior of San Marco.

A feast for the eyes The Chiostro di Sant' Antonino, the cloister through which you enter, is decorated with faded frescoes by Fra Angelico and other Florentine artists. In the Ospizio dei Pellegrini, where pilgrims were cared for, there is a superb collection of freestanding paintings by Fra Angelico and his followers. At the top of the staircase on the way to the dormitory is Fra Angelico's *Annunciation* (1440), an image of great tenderness and grace. Each of the 44 monks' cells is adorned with a small fresco by Fra Angelico or one of his assistants. The themes include the *Entombment* (cell 2) and the *Mocking of Christ* (cell 7). Savonarola's rooms house an exhibition about him. Cells 38 and 39 were reserved for Cosimo il Vecchio, who periodically spent time in the monastery.

THE BASICS

www.polomuseale.firenze.it
✚ G4
✉ Piazza San Marco 3
☎ 055 294 833
🕐 Church daily 7–12, 4–8.
Museum Mon–Fri 8.30–
1.50, Sat, Sun 8.15–4.50;
closed 1st, 3rd, 5th Sun,
2nd, 4th Mon of month
🚌 C1
♿ Acceptable
💰 Moderate

HIGHLIGHTS

● Fra Angelico's cell paintings
● Fra Angelico's *Annunciation*
● Savonarola's cells
● Cosimo il Vecchio's cells

Santa Maria Novella

Santa Maria Novella's facade (left) makes an ideal perch for passing visitors (right)

THE BASICS

www.chiesasantamaria novella.it

✚ E5

⊠ Piazza di Santa Maria Novella

☎ Church 055 219 257; Museum 055 282 187

🕐 Church Mon–Thu, Sat 9–5, Fri, Sun 1–5; closed during services. Museum Mon–Thu, Sat 9–5

🚆 5-min walk from the railway station

🚌 All buses to train station

♿ Good

💵 Church inexpensive; museum inexpensive

HIGHLIGHTS

● Marble facade
● Masaccio's *Trinità*
● Cappellone degli Spagnoli
● Tornabuoni Chapel
● Brunelleschi's wooden crucifix (1420) in Cappella Gondi

The decorative marble facade of Tuscany's most important Gothic church incorporates billowing sails (emblem of Alberti's patron, Rucellai) and ostrich feathers (emblem of the Medici).

Dominican origins The church of Santa Maria Novella was built between 1279 and 1357 by Dominican monks. The lower part of the marble facade, Romanesque in style, is believed to be by Fra Jacopo Talenti; the upper part was completed between 1456 and 1470 by Leon Battista Alberti.

Deceptive interior Inside, the church is vast and looks even longer than it is, thanks to the clever spacing of the columns. As you face the altar, on the left-hand side is Masaccio's fresco of the *Trinità* (c.1428), one of the earliest paintings to demonstrate mastery of perspective. Many of the chapels are named after the church's wealthy patrons. The Strozzi Chapel (left transept) is dedicated to St. Thomas Aquinas and decorated with frescoes (1351–57) by Nardo di Cione depicting *Heaven and Hell*: Dante himself is represented in the *Last Judgement* just behind the altar. The Tornabuoni Chapel contains Ghirlandaio's fresco cycle of the life of St. John the Baptist (1485) in contemporary costume. The Cappellone degli Spagnoli ('Spanish Chapel'), was used by the courtiers of Eleanor of Toledo, wife of Cosimo I. In the frescoes *Triumph of the Doctrine* (c.1365) by Andrea da Firenze, the dogs of God (a pun on the word Dominican—*domini canes*) are sent to round up lost sheep into the fold of the church.

A scene from *Life of Saint Benizzi (left) in Santissima Annunziata church (right)*

Santissima Annunziata

The intimacy and delicate architecture of the Piazza della SS. Annunziata contrast with the grandeur of much of Florence. The roundels of babies on the Ospedale degli Innocenti are quite enchanting.

Old New Year The Feast of the Annunciation on 25 March used to be New Year in the old Florentine calendar, and for that reason the church and the square have always played a special role in the life of the city. Every year, on 25 March, a fair is still held in the square and special biscuits called *brigidini* are sold.

Wedding flowers The church of Santissima Annunziata was built by Michelozzo in 1444–81 on the site of a Servite oratory. Entry is through an atrium known as the Chiostrino dei Voti (1447), which has the air of a rickety greenhouse, though the frescoes inside are superb. They include Rosso Fiorentino's *Assumption*, Pontormo's *Visitation* and Andrea del Sarto's *Birth of the Virgin*. The church is dedicated to the Virgin Mary, due to the legend that a painting of the Virgin was started by a monk in 1252 and finished by an angel. Newlyweds have traditionally brought their wedding bouquet to the church to ensure a happy marriage.

Early orphanage The Spedale degli Innocenti, on the east side of the piazza, was the first orphanage in Europe. A small museum includes works by major artists from the 14th to the 18th centuries. Designed by Brunelleschi in 1419, it has enamel terracotta roundels by della Robbia (1498).

THE BASICS

➕ G4
✉ Piazza della SS. Annunziata
☎ 055 266 181; Spedale degli Innocenti 055 203 7308
🕐 Daily 7.30–12.30, 4–6.30; closed during services. Spedale daily 8.30–7 (Sun until 2)
🚌 C1
♿ Good
🎟 Church free; Spedale moderate

HIGHLIGHTS

● Andrea della Robbia's roundels
● Facade of the Spedale degli Innocenti
● Rosso Fiorentino's *Assumption*
● Pontormo's *Visitation*
● Andrea del Sarto's *Birth of the Virgin*

More to See

GIARDINO DEI SEMPLICI

This oasis of neat greenery, the botanical garden of Florence University, is on the site of a garden laid out in 1545–46 for Cosimo I, who wanted to keep up with the Pisans and Genoans. It is named after the medicinal plants (*semplici*) grown here. There are also greenhouses with tropical palms, orchids and citrus fruits.

➕ G4 ✉ Via Micheli 3 ☎ 055 275 7402 🕐 Mar–Aug daily 10–7; Sep–Feb Sat–Mon 10–5 🚍 C1 ♿ Good 💷 Inexpensive

MERCATO CENTRALE

The largest of Florence's produce markets is held in the magnificent cast-iron structure of the Mercato Centrale, built in 1874, with an extra floor added in 1980.

➕ F4 ✉ Via dell'Ariento 🕐 Jul–Aug Mon–Sat 7–2; Sep–Jun Mon–Fri 7–2, Sat 7–5 🚍 All buses to Sta Maria Novella station ♿ Good (but crowded)

MERCATO SAN LORENZO

Fun, touristy and centrally located by the church of San Lorenzo. Lots of stalls sell leather goods. Many are genuinely good value, but go armed with a healthy scepticism.

➕ F5 ✉ Piazza San Lorenzo 🕐 Daily 9–7.30 🚍 C1, C2 ♿ Good

MUSEO ARCHEOLOGICO

One of the best places to see Etruscan art. There are also Roman, Greek and Egyptian exhibits. Notable is the rare collection from Kafiri, north Pakistan.

➕ H4 ✉ Palazzo della Crocetta, Via della Colonna 36 ☎ 055 23575 🕐 Tue–Fri 8.30–7, Sat–Mon 8.30–2 🚍 C1 ♿ Good 💷 Moderate

MUSEO BOTANICO

www.msn.unifi.it

A collection of Florence University, the museum, founded in 1842, houses 4 million specimens—the largest and most important collection of its kind in Italy. Be sure to see the Andrea Cesalpino Herbarium and the wax models of plants.

➕ G3 ✉ Via La Pira 4 ☎ 055 275 7462 🕐 By appointment only; call first 🚍 C2 ♿ Good 💷 Free

Artichokes for sale in the Mercato Centrale

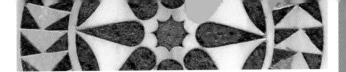

MUSEO DI LEONARDO DA VINCI

www.mostredileonardo.com

This exhibition complex is dedicated to the 'genius of Leonardo', with some 40 models of his inventions. Categories cover machines connected to the elements of earth, fire, water and air, with a fifth section on mechanical devices. Visitors can manoeuvre the machines, which have been reconstructed in wood, metal and textiles.

➕ G5 ✉ Via dei Servi 66–68 ☎ 055 282 966 🕐 Apr–Oct daily 10–7; Nov–Mar 10–6 🚇 C1 ♿ Good 💷 Expensive

MUSEO NAZIONALE DI ANTROPOLOGIA E ETNOLOGIA

www.msn.unifi.it

Founded in 1869 (part of Florence University), this museum offers more than just art and history. The people of the areas of Africa that came under Italian colonial rule are represented.

➕ G5 ✉ Palazzo Nonfinito, Via del Proconsolo 12 ☎ 055 239 6449 🕐 Mon–Tue, Thu–Fri 10–1, 4–7, Sat–Sun 10–7 🚇 C1, C2 ♿ Good 💷 Moderate

MUSEO STORICO TOPOGRAFICO (FIRENZE COM'ERA)

Paintings and maps in the collection show how Florence looked from the late 15th until the early 20th centuries. There are also 16th-century lunettes of the Medici villas, and the Pianta della Catena, an 1887 copy of a 1470 view of Florence.

➕ G5 ✉ Via dell'Oriuolo 24 ☎ 055 262 5961 🕐 Jun–Sep Mon–Tue 9–2, Sat 9–7; Oct–May Mon–Wed 9–2, Sat 9–7 🚇 C2 ♿ Good 💷 Inexpensive

SANTA MARIA MADDALENA DEI PAZZI

Although the original church dates from the 13th century, most of the present building is a Renaissance rebuild designed by Guiliano da Sangallo at the end of the 15th century. The spectacular interior decoration, with its marble and *trompe l'oeil*, dates from the baroque. The highlight here is in the fresco of the 1490s by Perugino in the chapter house (reached via the crypt).

➕ H5 ✉ Borgo Pinti 58 🕐 Daily 9–12, 5–9 🚇 C2, C3 ♿ Poor 💷 Inexpensive

Trompe l'oeil *in Santa Maria Maddalena dei Pazzi*

A large painted mummy case in the Museo Archeologico

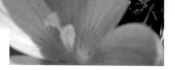

North of the City

Taking in Florence's main market area and the most important churches and galleries in the northern part of the city.

DISTANCE: 3km (2 miles) **ALLOW:** Full morning

START

CAPPELLE MEDICEE (▷ 57)
🚏 F5 🚌 C1

END

SANTISSIMA ANNUNZIATA (▷ 67)
🚏 G4 🚌 C1

1 Start at the Cappelle Medicee (▷ 57), in Piazza Madonna degli Aldobrandini, the last resting place of many of the Medici family.

8 Across the square is the Ospedale degli Innocenti. If time permits go inside to see the modest museum and the two Brunelleschi cloisters.

2 The church of San Lorenzo (▷ 64) itself (entered from Piazza San Lorenzo) is a masterpiece of Renaissance church design. Inside are works by Donatello.

7 This is one of the city's most distinctive squares. The square's church, Santissima Annunziata (▷ 67), is known for its frescoes by Andrea del Santo and others.

3 Explore the market north of San Lorenzo; cut through the Mercato Centrale (▷ 68) and return to Piazza San Lorenzo. The Palazzo Medici-Riccardi (▷ 63) is on the north side.

6 The ex-convent on the north side of the square houses Museo di San Marco (▷ 65), devoted to the works of Fra Angelico. Continue eastward along Via Cesare Battisti to Piazza della Santissima Annunziata.

4 Follow Via Cavour and take the second left into Via degli Arazzieri, follow into Via XXVII Aprile to reach the former convent of Sant' Apollonia, with a fresco of the Last Supper by Andrea del Castagno.

5 Walk east to Piazza San Marco, viewing Michelangelo's *David* in the Galleria dell'Accademia (▷ 60–61).

WALK

THE NORTH CENTRO

Shopping

ABACUS
www.abacusfirenze.it
The sign on the door says that this bookbindery aspires to 'sturdiness and beauty'. The hand-stitched spines and exquisitely lined covers make the volumes exceptional gifts. For such good quality, the prices are surprisingly low.
➕ F4 ✉ Via de'Ginori 28–30r ☎ 055 216 721 🚇 C1, C2

ALICE'S MASKS ART STUDIO
www.alicemasks.com
Papier-mâché in all shapes and sizes are here: animals—mythical and real—as well as more theatrical and surreal characters. They are all hand painted and finished.
➕ E4 ✉ Via Faenza 72r ☎ 055 287 370 🚇 C2

ARTE CRETA
Admire artist Elisabetta di Costanzo painting her majolica fresh from the kiln in brilliant hues. Her delightful pieces make a refreshing souvenir.
➕ G6 ✉ Via del Proconsolo 63r ☎ 055 284 341 🚇 C1, C2

BARTOLINI
www.dinobartolini.it
A Florentine institution; the junction where it stands is referred to as 'Bartolini Corner'. It sells just about every item of kitchenware you could wish for, as well as fine china and porcelain. All the worldwide names are

here but look out for the Italian ceramics such as Italian Arts and Solimene-Vietri ware.
➕ G5 ✉ Via dei Servi 30 ☎ 055 211 895 🚇 C1

BLUNAUTA
This Italian chain sells funky, casual clothing in natural fabrics that looks good on all generations.
➕ G5 ✉ Via del Proconsolo 69r ☎ 055 212 460 🚇 C1, C2

BORGO
www.borgovino.com
This small, tempting and well-stocked wine shop focusses on smaller local winemakers. Cheryl, the American lady who runs the shop with her Italian husband, is a font of knowledge. *Biscotti*, pasta and olive oil are also sold here.
➕ E5 ✉ Borgo San Lorenzo 20r ☎ 055 215 103 🚇 C1

BOTTEGA ORAFA PENKO
www.penkofirenze.it
Master goldsmith Paolo Penco makes beautiful

MARBLED PAPER
The skill of marbling paper was brought to Florence from Venice, where it had been learned from the East in the 12th century. Today's Florentine paper goods range greatly in price and quality, but even the inexpensive goods are attractive—and easily transported.

jewellery to order using techniques that originate from the Renaissance period.
➕ F5 ✉ Via F Zannetti 14 ☎ 055 211 661 🚇 C1

LA BOTTEGHINA DEL CERAMISTA
The vivid and lively patterns that are hand painted on these jugs, bowls and dishes at this shop will brighten any table.
➕ F4 ✉ Via Guelfa 5r ☎ 055 287 367 🚇 C2, D

CASA DEL VINO
www.casadelvino.it
This wine shop has occupied the same premises since it first opened in the second half of the 19th century. Today it has a very well-stocked cellar with nearly 1,000 wines from around the world. You are invited to sample wine by the glass and have a snack while deciding which bottle to buy.
➕ F4 ✉ Via dell'Ariento 16r ☎ 055 215 609 🚇 C2, D

CORNICI CAMPANI
This artisan shop has been dedicated to making handcrafted frames for paintings since 1889. The founder, Gino Campani, was a well-known collector and celebrated frame maker. Custom-made frames take approximately one week to complete.
➕ G5 ✉ Via dei Servi 22r ☎ 055 216 984 🚇 C1

ECHO

www.echofirenze.it

It's doubtful you'll have ever heard of any of the labels in this shop but you're sure to be bowled over by the clever designs. Go through the rails and check out the reasonable prices. A younger, funkier Echo is located next door.

⊞ G5 ✉ Via dell' Oriuolo 37–39r ☎ 055 238 1149 🚌 C2

ERMENI

www.erminiagostino.com

This bizarre fabric shop seems stuck in a time warp, but it's worth visiting for some good-value linen. There are also some more lavish fabrics for upholstering and soft furnishings.

⊞ F5 ✉ Via Borgo San Lorenzo 3r ☎ 055 292 200 🚌 C1

FRATELLI ALINARI

www.alinari.com

For the kind of postcards you want to keep rather than send, Alinari's, established in 1852, has an awesome archive that includes some of the first photographs ever taken in Italy. You can order any print for a very reasonable price. It also sells beautiful coffee-table books.

⊞ E5 ✉ Largo Alinari 15 ☎ 055 23951 🚌 C2, D

FRETTE

www.frette.com

This world-famous Italian company produces refined superior fabrics for the home, always at the cutting edge of fashion; bedding, tableware and lots more.

⊞ G4 ✉ Via Cavour 2r ☎ 055 211 369 🚌 C1

HERMÈS

www.hermes.com

This is the biggest and best equipped branch in Italy of the renowned Paris-based designer. Expect top-quality, classically elegant clothes.

⊞ E5 ✉ Piazza Antinori 6r ☎ 055 238 1004 🚌 C2

INTIMISSIMI

The simple cotton and silk lingerie and sleepwear is hard to beat in terms of quality and price. You can be assured a good service.

⊞ E5 ✉ Via de Cerretani 15r ☎ 055 239 9132 🚌 C2

SHOE CITY

The Florentines are famed for making superb shoes. As a testament to the historical importance of the industry in the city's economy, one of the main streets in Florence is named after the shoemakers (Calzaiuoli). The range of shoes available is vast, from the pinnacle of international chic to the value-for-money styles for sale in the market of San Lorenzo. Showrooms at the leather 'factories' in the Santa Croce area are worth a visit.

LIBRERIA ANTIQUARIA GONNELLI

www.gonnelli.it

For more than a century collectors have been coming to this historic bookshop to discover old and rare books, stamps and manuscripts.

⊞ G4 ✉ Via Ricasoli 14r ☎ 055 216 835 🚌 C1, C2

LORETTA CAPONI

www.lorettacaponi.com

Feminine linens, nightclothes and lingerie for mother and daughter.

⊞ E5 ✉ Piazza Antinori 4r ☎ 055 213 668 🚌 C2

MAXMARA

www.maxmara.com

Classic elegance takes precedence over ostentation; clothes are of superb quality, beautifully tailored and at reasonable prices.

⊞ F5 ✉ Via dei Pecori 23r ☎ 055 287 761 🚌 C2

ORNAMENTA

This little shop sells small amber rings and silver earrings along with more ethnic styles at affordable prices.

⊞ G5 ✉ Via Proconsolo 65 ☎ 055 292 879 🚌 C1, C2

OSTERIA DE L'ORTOLANO

www.osteriafirenze.com

A must for fans of Italian food, this excellent delicatessen and catering company has been in business since 1962. Pick up a complete meal to take out or choose from

the array of biscuits, jams and sauces for a souvenir to bring home.

🔢 G5 ✉ Via degli Alfani 91r ☎ 055 239 6466 🚌 C2

IL PAPIRO

www.ilpapirofierenze.it

These shops in central Florence sell excellent marbled paper goods in particularly pretty shades. These include little chests of drawers and tiny jewellery boxes. At four other locations in the city.

🔢 G4 ✉ Via Cavour 59r ☎ 055 215 262 🚌 C1

PASSAMANERIA TOSCANA FIRENZE

www.ptfsrl.com

This shop sells furnishing fabrics, brocades, tassels and other trimmings as well as cushions and footstools. The shades and textures are rich and sensuous, the whole experience bordering on the utterly abandoned.

🔢 F5 ✉ Piazza San Lorenzo 12r ☎ 055 214 670 🚌 C1

LE PIETRE NELL'ARTE

www.scarpellimosaici.it

A really classy shop run by the Scarpelli family. They sell beautiful hard and semiprecious stone inlays, interior decorations and artistic objects including sculptures, tables, pictures, brooches and much more. The stones used included onyx, chalcedony, malachite and jasper.

🔢 F5 ✉ Piazza Duomo 36r ☎ 055 212 587 🚌 C1, C2

RASPINI

www.raspini.com

A few steps from the Duomo, this fashion store is known for giving a platform to new young designers, and there is no shortage of prestigious labels on offer. There are also branches at Via Roma 25r and Via Por Santa Maria 72r, and Raspini Vintage at Via Calimaruzza 17r.

🔢 F5 ✉ Via Martelli 5–7r ☎ 055 239 8336 🚌 C1, C2

RICHARD GINORI

Florence's own porcelain designer, who also does dinner services to order with your family crest, a picture of your home or whatever else you want.

🔢 E5 ✉ Via Rondinelli 17r ☎ 055 210 041 🚌 C2

SBIGOLI TERRECOTTE

www.sbigoliterrecotte.it

Pots designed, painted and fired in Florence by the family owners, whose workshop can be visited behind the shop. The designs, based mainly on ones popular in the Renaissance, come in majolica and tactile unglazed terracotta, and at good prices.

🔢 G5 ✉ Via Sant'Egidio 4r ☎ 055 247 9713 🚌 C1

SCRIPTORIUM

www.scriptoriumfirenze.com

This shop draws on two great Florentine crafts—leather working and paper making—to create objects of beauty and refined taste. The plain paper books are notable, bound with soft leather in subdued natural shades.

🔢 G5 ✉ Via dei Servi 5–7r ☎ 055 211 804 🚌 C1

TERRE DEI GIGLI

www.terredeigigli.it

The best virgin olive oil, Tuscan ragu, *crostini* and *cantuccini* biscuits are just a sample of the Tuscan fare crammed into this tiny deli, which is housed in a historic palazzo.

🔢 F4 ✉ Via de' Ginori 21r ☎ 055 260 8659 🚌 C1, C2

ZANOBINI

Part traditional bar, part wine shop, Zanobini's is patronzied by locals. Stop by for a drink and a snack while you buy your wine.

🔢 F4 ✉ Via Sant'Antonino 47r ☎ 055 239 6850 🚌 C1

Entertainment and Nightlife

ASTOR CAFFÈ

Stylish café/bar serving up Mediterranean dishes accompanied by a house, jazz or easy-listening soundtrack. Grab a seat for an *apertivo* and munch on the buffet snacks before the DJ gets going in the back room.

➕ F5 ✉ Piazza Duomo 20r ☎ 055 284 305 🚌 C1, C2

JAZZ CLUB

www.jazzclubfirenze.it

A popular venue among jazz aficionados. Although technically a private club, it is very easy to become a member (▷ panel). If you like live jazz and a relaxed atmosphere, then this is the place for you.

➕ H5 ✉ Via Nuova dei Caccini 3 ☎ 055 247 9700 🕐 Closed Mon, Sun and Jun–Sep 🚌 C1

LYCEUM

www.lyceumclubfirenze.net

The Lyceum presents an occasional schedule of chamber music and classical recitals in elegant surroundings.

➕ G5 ✉ Via degli Alfani 48r ☎ 055 247 8264 🚌 C1, C2

OPERA ET GUSTO

This is a novel way to spend an evening, combining a first-class meal with music, dance and theatre. The tables are arranged at the foot of the stage and red velvet curtains encircle the room creating an intimate, warm feel. After the performance the venue transforms into an open bar with live music.

➕ E5 ✉ Via della Scala 17r ☎ 055 288 190 🕐 Show 8pm–10.45pm. Bar until 2am 🚌 C2

PALESTRA RICCIARDI

www.palestraricciardi.it

The oldest, biggest and most central gym in the city, founded some 50 years ago, with all the latest equipment.

➕ H4 ✉ Borgo Pinti 75 ☎ 055 247 8444 🚌 C2

REX CAFÈ

A popular bar with a spellbinding interior of retro lighting and paint-splashed walls. Open until 2.30am.

➕ H5 ✉ Via Fiesolana 23r ☎ 055 248 0331 🚌 C1, C2

SPACE ELECTRONIC

www.spaceclubfirenze.com

Upstairs you'll find a vast dance floor, where an eclectic selection of music is played, ranging from up-to-the-minute hits to 1950s and 60s classics. Noisy and very popular with tourists.

➕ D5 ✉ Via Palazzuolo 37 ☎ 055 293 082 🚌 D

TEATRO COMUNALE

www.maggiofiorentino.com

The largest of Florence's concert halls—the main venue of the Maggio Musicale in spring and the festival's box office—also has its own classical season. The Ridotto, or Piccolo, is the theatre's smaller auditorium.

➕ C5 ✉ Corso Italia 16 ☎ Box office 055 277 9350 🚌 C2, C3, D

TEATRO DELLA PERGOLA

www.fondazioneteatro dellapergola.it

Well-known productions are regularly held in the sumptuous surroundings of the two elegant halls. This is one of the city's most important venues for classical music, with some Maggio Musicale concerts held here.

➕ G5 ✉ Via della Pergola 12–32 ☎ 055 22641 🚌 C1, C2

CLUBS ITALIAN STYLE

Many clubs and music venues (and even a few bars and restaurants) are private clubs or *associazione culturale*. This doesn't mean that visitors are unwelcome but rather that it's easier for them to get a licence as a club than as a public *locale*. It's really very easy to become a member; you may be charged a euro or so over and above the official entry price, but it's still worth doing even if you're only going to use your membership once. Many clubs actually have free membership. All you need to do is fill in your name, address, date of birth and sometimes occupation on a form and you'll be presented with a membership card.

Restaurants

PRICES

Prices are approximate, based on a 3-course meal for one person.

€€€	over €55
€€	€35–€55
€	under €35

BELCORE (€€)

www.ristorantebelcore.it
Enjoy refined modern Italian cooking in tranquil, elegant surroundings. The plain cream walls provide a stage for the work of up-and-coming artists. There is an impressive wine list with more than 300 wines to choose from.
🚩 D5 ✉ Via dell'Albero 30 ☎ 055 211 198 🕐 Closed lunch Tue, Wed 🚌 C2, D

CANTINETTA ANTINORI (€€€)

www.cantinetta-antinori.com
A refined setting for the chic Florentine elite. The food comes from the farm of the Antinori family, whose wines are world renowned. The wonderful dishes use the best seasonal produce. Dress up or you are likely to feel completely out of place.
🚩 E5 ✉ Piazza Antinori 3 ☎ 055 292 234 🕐 Closed Sat, Sun, Aug 🚌 C2

COQUINARIUS (€€)

www.coquinarius.com
This restaurant-cum-wine bar full of dark wood and stylish posters is a great place to sample differ-ent cheeses, cold cuts, smoked fish, *carpacci*

meats and *stuzzichini* (Italian bar snacks), and exceptionally good cakes.
🚩 F5 ✉ Via delle Oche 15r ☎ 055 230 2153 🕐 Closed Sun 🚌 C1

GELATERIA CARABÉ (€)

www.gelatocarabe.com
A top-quality Sicilian ice-cream store run with great pride by Antonio and Loredana Lisciandro. *The place to have a *granita* (ice slush) in Florence, or try the *cremolata* made from the fruit pulp, includ-ing melon and blackberry. No artificial ingredients are added to the products.
🚩 G4 ✉ Via Ricasoli 60r ☎ 055 289 476 🚌 C1, C2

LA GIOSTRA (€€€)

www.ristorantelagiostra.com
Prepare to be spoiled at this enclave of fine dining, owned by a Hapsburg

ITALIAN CAKES

There are three main types of Tuscan cake. *Brioche* (pastries) are made with sweet yeast dough and filled with oozing custard. *Torte* (cakes) tend to be tarts, such as the ubiquitous *torta della nonna* (granny's cake), a kind of cake in tart form, or *torta di ricotta*, in which ricotta is mixed with sugar and candied peel. Then there are all kinds of little cookies, most of which contain nuts and have names like *brutti ma buoni* (ugly but good).

prince and run by his daughter and twin sons. Upon entering, you are offered a crystal flute of *spumante*, which prepares you for the refined menu. The home-made pasta courses are divine and the mains are equally imagi-native and exquisite. Save room for the Viennese *Sachertorte*. Twinkling lights decorate the cosy dining room, which is surmounted by 16th-century brick arches.
🚩 G5 ✉ Borgo Pinti 10r ☎ 055 241 341 🚌 C1, C2

GOZZI SERGIO (€)

A basic but good trattoria with a daily changing menu. Hidden behind the Mercato San Lorenzo, it is not the easiest place to find and it's only open for lunch, but it's worth a detour.
🚩 F5 ✉ Piazza San Lorenzo 8r ☎ 055 281 941 🕐 Closed dinner, Sun, Aug 🚌 C2, D

LE MOSSACCE (€–€€)

www.trattorialemossacce.it
Bustling eatery between the Duomo and the Bargello. Excellent Tuscan food including rich soup.
🚩 G6 ✉ Via del Proconsolo 55r ☎ 055 294 361 🕐 Closed Sat, Sun, Aug 🚌 C1, C2

PALLE D'ORO (€)

Spotless and spartan, this restaurant serves good food and is excel-lent value. Expect hearty soups, gnocchi dumpling

dishes, decent fish and filling pasta servings. Adequate wine list.

🔷 F4 ✉ Via Sant'Antonino 27r ☎ 055 288 383 🕐 Closed Sun 🚇 C1

RELAIS LE JARDIN (€€€)

The dark wood and carpeted interiors, and the lush well-kept gardens give the Hotel Regency's restaurant a British feel. Immaculately prepared and presented menu. Reserve early to ensure a candlelit table.

🔷 H5 ✉ Piazza Massimo D'Azeglio ☎ 055 245 247 🚇 C1, C2, C3

ROBIGLIO (€€)

www.robiglio.it

The old-fashioned Florentine bar/*pasticceria* par excellence opened its first branch in 1928. The pastries are to die for.

🔷 F5 ✉ Via Tosinghi 11r ☎ 055 215 013 🚇 C1

RUTH'S (€)

www.kosheruth.com

A bright, modern Jewish restaurant next to the synagogue serving an interesting mix of vegetarian (although fish is also served), Middle Eastern and kosher food.

🔷 H5 ✉ Via Farini 2a ☎ 055 248 0888 🕐 Closed Fri dinner, Sat lunch 🚇 C2, C3

SABATINI (€€€)

www.ristorantesabatini.it

This elegant, wood-filled restaurant is a respected Florentine stalwart. Particularly good for local steak and an excellent seafood risotto.

🔷 E5 ✉ Via dei Panzani 9a ☎ 055 282 802 🕐 Closed Mon 🚇 C2

TAVERNA DEL BRONZINO (€€–€€€)

Here you will find a wealth of Tuscan culinary delights such as smoked goose breast with olive oil. If available, and you love fish, try the expertly prepared sea bass. Expect excellent service.

🔷 F3 ✉ Via delle Ruote 27r ☎ 055 495 220 🕐 Closed Sun, Aug 🚇 C2

TRATTORIA ANTELLESI (€€)

www.trattoriaantellesi.com

A great place for a vegetarian to join a meat-eating friend. Good range

of inventive starters and delicious main courses— the *peposo alla fiorentina* (a peppery beef stew in red wine) is very tasty. There is a decent wine list and a traditional Florentine dessert made with chestnuts.

🔷 E4 ✉ Via Faenza 9r ☎ 055 216 990 🕐 Closed Tue 🚇 C2

TRATTORIA ANTICHI CANCELLI (€)

You can expect hearty Tuscan food at this mainstay trattoria. There is a good selection for vegetarians on the mixed menu, including hearty soups, *contorni* (side dishes) and the classic spaghetti *pomodoro e basilico* (tomato and basil). The house wine is good value.

🔷 E4 ✉ Via Faenza 73r ☎ 055 218 927 🕐 Closed Mon 🚇 C2

ZÀ-ZÀ (€–€€)

www.trattoriazaza.it

An old-fashioned, inexpensive trattoria near the Mercato Centrale, which is very popular with visitors. The Tuscan food is excellent, and the fixed-price menus are great value. The inviting stone-walled interior is especially appealing in the summer heat. It's best to arrive at opening time or reserve a table.

🔷 F4 ✉ Piazza del Mercato Centrale 26r ☎ 055 215 411 🕐 Closed Sun (except last Sun of month) 🚇 C2

Literally translated as 'beyond the Arno', the Oltrarno is the site of the Pitti Palace and the Boboli Gardens. It is also the most relaxed part of the city, least touched by tourism and with some of the best views.

4

5

6

LUNGARNO SODERINI

Piazza
di Cestello
✝ San Frediano
in Cestello

Piazza
N Sauro

LUNGARNO GUICCIARDINI

BORGO SAN FREDIANO

SERRAGLI

Via Guicciardini

Palazzo
Guicciardini

Palazzo
Frescobaldi

Palazzo
Frescobaldi

Piazza del
Borgo d Stella

Via S Monaca

✝

Spirito Frescobaldi

Borgo San Jacopo

Piazza
di Santa
Felicita

**Cappella
Brancacci** ●

Via S Agostino

Via dell'Anguillara

**SANTO
SPIRITO**

✝

Mattia

**Santo
Spirito** ●

Via il Prato di Mezzo

Palazzo
Firidolfi

Via de' Guicciardini

Piazza
di Santa Mar
Soprarno

Santa Maria
del Carmine

Piazza
S Spirito

Fognolo

Via Romana

Palazzo
Corsini

Maggio

Via de' Bardi

Costa

**Santa
Felicita** ✝

San
Girolamo

7

*Giardino
Torrigiani*

✝

Via della Chiesa

Borgo Campuccio

Via Santa Maria

Via Mazzetta

Sdrucciolo

Piazza
S Felice

Palazzo
de' Pitti

**Galleria del
Costume** ●

✝

Santo
Spirito
della Calza

VIALE FRANCESCO PETRARCA

Via del SERRAGLI

Via de

Palazzo
Torrigiani

Piazza
S Felice

**Palazzo
Pitti** ●

Vicolo

8

P

P

Porta
Romana

Piazzale di
Porta Romana

VIALE

NICCOLÒ

**Museo della
Specola** ●

*Giardino
di Bòboli*

Viale dei Cipressi

**Galleria d'Arte
Moderna** ●

Fonte
del Nettuno

**Museo delle
Porcellane** ●

**Forte di
Belvedere** ●

Via San Leonardo

9

0   250 m
0   250 yds

Istituto
d'Arte

✝

Via d Mascherino

Via d Madonna
della Pace

Via di Belvedere

Via di Bobolino

BOBOLINO

MACHIAVELLI

✝ S Leonardo
in Arcetri

C   **D**   **E**   **F**

Ponte alle Grazie

Arno

Ch Tedesca

ngarno Torrigiani

Bardi

LUNGARNO

Palazzo Serristori

Palazzo de' Mozzi

Via del Renai

Via del Giardino Serristori

SERRISTORI

LUNGARNO BENVENUTO CELLINI

Museo Bardini

Via di

San Niccolò

Via S. Niccolò

P

Porta San Niccolò

Via a Fornace

Palazzo Torrigiani

Piazza G Poggi

Via dei Bastioni

Palazzi de' Mozzi

SAN NICCOLÒ

Via di Belvedere

Via del Monte alle Croci

Viale Giuseppe Poggi

David

Piazzale Michelangelo

Camping Michelangelo

VIALE MICHELANGIOLO

Via di San Miniato al monte

Via

Via dell'Erta

Convento delle Stimmatine

San Salvatore al Monte

Via del Mte alle Croci

Canina

GALILEO

San Miniato al Monte

Viuzzo delle Corti

Cimitero delle Porte Sante

Via delle Porte Sante

Passo all'Erta

GALILEO

Viuzzo di Cartaia

Via del Salviatino

VIALE

G   H   J

Cappella Brancacci

Part of the thrill of the Cappella Brancacci is observing in Masaccio's frescoes the power of expression and technical brilliance that inspired the Florentine painters of the 15th century.

Miniature gem This tiny chapel is reached via the cloisters of the otherwise rather dull Santa Maria del Carmine. Two layers of frescoes commissioned in 1424 by Felice Brancacci, a wealthy Florentine merchant and statesman, illustrate the life of St. Peter, shown in his orange gown. The frescoes were designed by Masolino da Panicale, who began painting them with his brilliant pupil, Masaccio. In 1428 Masaccio took over from Masolino but died that year, aged 27; the rest of the frescoes were completed in the 1480s by Filippino Lippi.

Restoration revelations In the 1980s the chapel was restored, with the removal of accumulated candle soot and layers of an 18th-century egg-based gum (which had formed a mould). The frescoes now have an intense radiance that makes it possible to see very clearly the shifts in emphasis between Masolino's work and that of Masaccio; contrast the serenity of Masolino's *Temptation of Adam and Eve* with the excruciating agony of Masaccio's *Expulsion of Adam and Eve from Paradise*. The restoration has also highlighted Masaccio's mastery of chiaroscuro (light and shade), which, combined with his grasp of perspective, was marvelled at and consciously copied by 15th-century Florentine painters.

THE BASICS

www.museicivicifiorentini.it/brancacci

➕ D6

✉ Santa Maria del Carmine, Piazza del Carmine (enter through the cloisters)

☎ 055 276 8558; 055 276 8224 (advance reservations mandatory)

🕐 Mon, Wed–Sat 10–5, Sun 1–5. Entrance by reservation only

🚌 6, D

♿ Poor

✋ Moderate

HIGHLIGHTS

● Masaccio's *Expulsion of Adam and Eve from Paradise*
● Masaccio's *St. Peter heals the Sick*
● Filippino Lippi's *St. Paul visits St. Peter in Prison*
● Masaccio's *Tribute Money*

OLTRARNO

★ **TOP 25**

Giardino di Boboli

Views and fountains abound in the Boboli Gardens, a welcome haven

THE BASICS

www.polomuseale.firenze.it
🔲 E8
✉ Piazza Pitti
☎ 055 238 8786
🕐 Jun–Aug daily 8.15–7.30; Apr–May, Sep–Oct 8.15–6.30; Mar 8.15–5.30; Nov–Feb 8.15–4.30; closed 1st and last Mon of month
🚌 D
♿ Good; some steps
💶 Expensive, includes Gardens, Museo delle Porcellane, Galleria del Costume (both ▷ 86) and Museo degli Argenti (▷ 85)

HIGHLIGHTS

● Bacchus fountain (1560)
● La Grotta Grande, a Mannerist cave-cum-sculpture gallery (1583–88)
● Views of the hills from the Giardino dei Cavalieri
● Limonaia (1785)—protected trees from the frost; now a huge garden shed
● The Isolotto

The Boboli Gardens are, quite literally, a breath of fresh air. They are the only easily accessible reservoir of greenery and tranquillity in Florence, and a lovely retreat after a hard day's sightseeing.

Renaissance origins The Boboli Gardens were created for the Medici when they moved to the Palazzo Pitti in 1550. They represent a superb example of Italian Renaissance gardening, an interplay between nature and artifice expressed in a geometrical arrangement of fountains, grass and low box hedges. In 1766 they were opened to the public, and in 1992 an (unpopular) entrance charge was imposed.

Amphitheatre Just behind the Palazzo Pitti is the amphitheatre, built where the stone for the palazzo was quarried. It was the site of the first-ever opera performance and is surrounded by mazelike alleys of fragrant, dusty bay trees. Go uphill past the Neptune Fountain (1565–68) to reach the Giardino dei Cavalieri, where roses and peonies wilt in the summer sun. The pretty building nearby houses the Museo delle Porcellane (Porcelain Museum, ▷ 86).

More to see The Viottolone, an avenue of cypresses planted in 1637 and studded with classical statues, leads to the Isolotto, an island set in a murky green pond dotted with pleasantly crumbling statues. In the middle is a copy of Giambologna's *Oceanus* fountain (1576), the original of which is in the Bargello (▷ 24–25).

Crowds flock up the steps of San Miniato al Monte to view its glorious mosaics

San Miniato al Monte

San Miniato is a wonderful sight on the hill above Florence, its marble facade glistening in the sunlight. Close up it is even more appealing, a jewel of the Romanesque inside and outside.

Christian martyr San Miniato (St. Minias) was an early Christian martyr who came to Florence from the Levant in the third century and was martyred in the Roman amphitheatre that stood on the site of today's Piazza della Signoria, by order of the Emperor Decius. It is said that his decapitated body picked up his head and walked into the hills. His shrine, the site of the present church, was built where he finally collapsed. The church was initially run by Benedictine monks, then by Cluniacs, and finally, from 1373 to the present day, by the Olivetans. In the Benedictine shop, on the right as you exit, monks sell honey and herbal potions.

An eagle visitation The church was built in 1018, with a green-and-white marble facade added at the end of the 11th century and mosaics in the 13th century. On the pinnacle a gilded copper statue of an eagle carries a bale of cloth (1410): This is the symbol of the Arte di Calimala, the wool importers' guild, which supported the church in the Middle Ages.

Miraculous crucifix Inside, an inlaid floor (*c.*1207) incorporates zodiac and animal themes. In the nave is a chapel (1448) by Michelozzo, built to house a miraculous crucifix that is now in Santa Trinità.

THE BASICS

- ➕ H9
- ✉ Via Monte alle Croce, off Viale Galileo Galilei
- ☎ 055 234 2731
- 🕐 Apr–Oct daily 8–8; Nov–Mar 8–1, 3.30–7; closed during services
- 🚌 12, 13
- ♿ Poor (make enquires)
- 🎟 Free

HIGHLIGHTS

- ● Marble facade
- ● Inlaid floor
- ● Mosaics in the apse
- ● Cappella del Crocifisso
- ● Wooden ceiling
- ● Cardinal of Portugal Chapel (1473)

Palazzo Pitti

- Frescoed ceilings by Pietro da Cortona, Galleria Palatina
- Raphael's *Madonna of the Chair* (c.1516)
- Titian's overtly sexual *Mary Magdalene* (c.1531)
- Van Dyck's *Charles I and Henrietta Maria* (c.1632)
- Titian's *Portrait of a Gentleman* (1540)

TIPS

- It makes sense to concentrate on the Galleria Palatina before moving on to another gallery.
- Be prepared for crowds, and sections to be closed.
- Book ahead to avoid disappointment.
- Leave time to relax afterwards in the Giardino di Boboli (▷ 82). Combined tickets can be bought.

The Pitti Palace, with its eight museums and galleries, is unremittingly grandiose and opulent, an architectural complex celebrating the power and wealth of the Medici, Florence's ruling family.

The building The wealthy banker, Luca Pitti, a business rival of the Medici, commissioned architect Filippo Brunelleschi to design a vast palazzo for his family in 1457. A century later, in 1549, the Pitti coffers were empty and the palace, ironically, was purchased by Eleonora de' Medici. The Medici family installed their art collections and expanded these, and the palazzo, right up until Italian unification in 1860.

The paintings The Galleria Palatina houses the picture collection, comprising works as

Clockwise from left: Cortona's ceiling fresco in the Sala di Marte inside the Palazzo Pitti's Palatine Gallery depicts the Roman God of War; the home of the Medici family for three centuries, the imposing Palazzo Pitti was designed in 1458 and enlarged in the 16th century; Palazzo Pitti seen from Giardino di Boboli

important as those in the Uffizi and still hung in tiers, as they would have been in the 18th century. Masterpieces hang side by side with less important works, and some paintings are difficult to see. Amidst the jumble, you'll find major works by Filipp Lippi and Raphael, two superb paintings by Titian and a dramatic Caravaggio.

Other collections The Galleria leads to the stunningly extravagant and beautifully restored Appartamenti Reali (State Rooms), a chain of interconnecting rooms running along one side of the palazzo. These are followed by the and the Museo degli Argenti (Silver Museum), with a collection of luxury items that are often a triumph of wealth over good taste. Elsewhere, you'll find the Galleria del Costume (▷ 86) and the Galleria d'Arte Moderna (▷ 86).

THE BASICS

www.polomuseale.firenze.it
➕ E7
✉ Piazza Pitti
☎ Galleria Palatina 055 238 8614; reservations 055 294 833
🕐 Galleria Palatina Tue–Sun 8.15–6.50; closed Jan. Argenti (▷ 82; same as Giardino di Boboli)
🚌 D
♿ Good
🎫 Galleria Palatina, Royal Apartments expensive; Galleria d'Arte Moderna combined ticket expensive; Museo degli Argenti (▷ 82, Boboli Gardens)

More to See

FORTE DI BELVEDERE

This was built by the Medici in 1590 as a refuge for the Medici Grand Dukes in their struggle against the Florentine Republic, and as a reminder of Medici military might. Occasional exhibitions are held here.

➕ F8 ✉ Via San Leonardo ☎ 055 262 5962 ⏰ View from the road 🚌 D, plus walk 🎫 Free

GALLERIA D'ARTE MODERNA

www.polomuseale.firenze.it

More than 30 rooms of artworks here span the mid-18th to mid-20th centuries. In the main building of the Palazzo Pitti on the floor above the Palatina.

➕ E7 ✉ Palazzo Pitti, Piazza Pitti ☎ 055 238 8616 ⏰ Tue–Sun 8.15–6.50 🚌 D ♿ Good 🎫 Inclusive ticket with Galleria Palatina (▷ 84) expensive

GALLERIA DEL COSTUME

www.polomuseale.firenze.it

One for devotees to clothes and fashion. The collection illustrates the history of costume from the

18th century up until the 1920s. Displays change frequently, and the gallery hosts many special exhibitions. In the Palazzina Meridiana in the south wing of the Palazzo Pitti.

➕ E7 ✉ Palazzo Pitti, Piazza Pitti ☎ 055 238 8713 ⏰ Giardino di Boboli (▷ 82, panel) 🚌 D ♿ Good 🎫 Inclusive ticket with Museo degli Argenti, Museo delle Porcellane, Giardino di Boboli expensive

MUSEO DELLE PORCELLANE

www.polomuseale.firenze.it

French, Italian, German and Viennese porcelain and ceramics in a pavilion at the top of the Giardino di Boboli.

➕ E8 ✉ Palazzo Pitti, Piazza Pitti ☎ 055 238 8709 ⏰ Giardino di Boboli (▷ 82, panel) 🚌 D ♿ Good, some steps 🎫 Inclusive ticket Museo degli Argenti, Museo delle Porcellane, Giardino di Boboli expensive

MUSEO DELLA SPECOLA

La Specola is so called after the observatory that used to be sited here. The museum of zoology and natural history is part of the university. An

Museo delle Porcellane

Defensive position—Forte di Belvedere

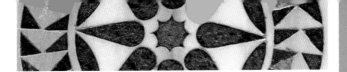

unusual highlight is the Cere Anatomiche, a gruesome set of 18th-century wax models of bits of human bodies. Also hundreds of skeletons and stuffed animals are on show.

🔲 E7 ✉ Via Romana 17 ☎ 055 228 8251 🕐 Tue–Sun 9.30–4.30 🚌 11, D ♿ Good 🎟 Expensive

PIAZZALE MICHELANGELO

Despite the fact that Piazzale Michelangelo is frequented by busloads of tourists, this stupendous vantage point is still very much worth the trip, either by bus or on foot. Ignore the poor green copy of Michelangelo's *David* and crop of souvenir stalls, beware of pickpockets and soak up the wonderful view.

🔲 H8 ✉ Viale Galileo Galilei 🚌 12, 13 ♿ Good 🎟 Free

PONTE ALLE GRAZIE

Dating from 1237, when it was known as Ponte Rubaconte (the bridge over the River Rubicon), the bridge was rebuilt to its 18th-century design after World War II. Its name is from the

oratory of Santa Maria delle Grazie, which once stood here.

🔲 G7 🚌 C3, D

SANTA FELICITA

This is the second-oldest church in Florence, dating to the second century AD. The highlight is the Mannerist *Deposition* (1525–28) by Pontormo, in the Cappella Caponi, immediately on your right as you enter. It is a stunning vortex of improbable forms and hues: lime green, bubblegum pink, acid yellow.

🔲 F7 ✉ Piazza Santa Felicita 🕐 055 213 018 🕐 Mon–Sat 9–12, 3.30–5.30. Closed Sun and during services. Mass: Sun 9, 11, Mon–Sat 6pm 🚌 D ♿ Poor 🎟 Free

SANTO SPIRITO

Designed by Filippo Brunelleschi in 1435, with an 18th-century baroque facade, which was never finished. The *cenacolo* (refectory) houses a fresco of the Last Supper by Nardo di Clone.

🔲 E7 ✉ Piazza Santo Spirito ☎ 055 210 030 🕐 Thu–Tue 10–12.30, 4–5.30 (not during services) 🚌 D ♿ Poor 🎟 Free

Get a great view from Piazzale Michelangelo

Around Oltrarno

Begin amid the bustle of Oltrarno, yet you're soon among tranquil surroundings to catch a glimpse of local life and see great views.

DISTANCE: 2km (1 mile) **ALLOW:** 2–3 hours

START .... **END**

PONTE VECCHIO (▷ 34) **PIAZZALE MICHELANGELO** (▷ 87)
➕ F7 🚌 C3 ➕ H8 🚌 12, 13

❶ In summer this walk can be baking hot; start early in the morning or after 4pm and take a bottle of water. Plan a midday picnic at the Forte di Belvedere (▷ 86).

❽ Continue downhill to Piazzale Michelangelo for great views. A No. 12 bus will take you back down to Ponte alle Grazie (▷ 87).

❷ Set off from the south side of the Ponte Vecchio (▷ 34–35) in Oltrarno. With your back to the bridge, take the first square on your left, Piazza di Santa Felicita.

❼ A little way up take the steep Via di San Salvadore al Monte on the left, which crosses Viale Galileo Galilei. Climb the hill flanked by cypress trees that continues up toward San Miniato (▷ 83). Return to Viale Galileo Galilei and go right.

❸ Here you will find Pontormo's *Deposition* in Santa Felicita (▷ 87) church. Take the road on the left of the church, the Costa di San Giorgio, where Galileo lived at No. 19.

❻ After the entrance to Fort Belvedere, descend steeply along the 13th-century defensive city walls. At the bottom of the hill, by the small gateway of Porta San Miniato, turn right and head up Via del Monte alle Croci.

❹ Continue up its steep slope. At the top, you pass through Porta di San Giorgio (1260), the oldest city gate, with a carving of St. George slaying the dragon.

❺ Follow Via del Belvedere, and leave the 1590 Forte di Belvedere on your right.

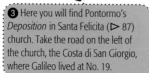

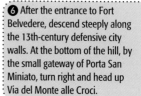

OLTRARNO WALK

Shopping

ALCOZER & J
www.alcozer.it
Sells quirky stylish pieces in a modern idiom using interesting metals and bright stones; costume brooches, necklaces and other items of jewellery.
➕ E7 ✉ Via Mannelli 15r
☎ 055 623 6346 🖥 D

ANNA
www.annapitti.it
This shop is in a 300-year-old tower in front of the Pitti Palace. Anna sells a great range of leather goods, bags, knitwear, cashmere, scarves and ties. A good place for men and women to shop in a quieter part of town.
➕ E7 ✉ Piazza Pitti 38–40r
☎ 055 283 787 🖥 D

ANTICO SETIFICIO FIORENTINO
www.setificiofiorentino.it
Ring the doorbell to gain access to this old Florentine silk factory that provides fabric for some of Italy's most sought-after designers. Much of the fabric is woven using traditional methods and 18th-century looms.
➕ C6 ✉ Via Lorenzo Bartolini 4 ☎ 055 213 861 🖥 D

BARTOLOZZI & MAIOLI
This antiques shop gives an insight into the Florentine love of ostentatious adornment. As you wander you can hear craftsmen tapping. Good pieces, but expensive.

➕ E7 ✉ Via Maggio 13r
☎ 055 239 8633 🖥 D

BOTTEGA DEL MOSAICO
www.bottegadelmosaico.com
The art of the Florentine mosaic, an inlay of hard and semiprecious stones, is unique in the world. The art has been practised for more than 500 years and it flourished at the court of the Medicis. Stones used range from agate to malachite. Examples can be seen in the world's most prestigious museums, including the Uffizi Gallery (▷ 28–29).
➕ E7 ✉ Via Guicciardini 126r ☎ 055 210 718
🖥 D

> ### POTTERY FACTS
> Traditional Italian ceramics are majolica, terracotta covered with a brilliant tin-based glaze. Arabic ceramics inspired pots made for the Medici court at Montelupo, near Florence. Deruta in Umbria makes flowery designs in blue on white or yellow. Designs in turquoise on white are also much in evidence. Tuscan peasant wares, white or yellow, splashed with green or blue spots, are increasingly popular. Among the best-known classic designs is Gran Faenza, with green, red and blue floral designs on a pale grey-blue background. Most shops offer shipping.

BOTTEGA DELLE STAMPE
www.bottegadellestampe.com
Framed and unframed antique or art nouveau prints (known in Italian as Liberty). Elegant.
➕ E6 ✉ Borgo San Jacopo 56r ☎ 055 295 396 🖥 D

LA CASA DELLA STAMPA
Vivianna is the lithographer who hand-tints many of these beautiful prints. There is a huge selection of Florentine scenes, from the Medici era to the early 19th century, and richly painted studies of butterflies and plants.
➕ E7 ✉ Sdrucciolo de Pitti 11r ☎ No phone 🖥 D

ENOTECA PERI
A no-nonsense wine and oil shop selling good-quality products. It lies just over the Santa Trinità bridge.
➕ E7 ✉ Via Maggio 5r
☎ 055 212 674 🖥 D

FARMACIA PITTI
It's worth walking through this former 15th-century herbalist shop just to see the sales room at the back decked out with antique glass jars and old cabinets. A modern working pharmacy serves your needs, too.
➕ E7 ✉ Piazza San Felice 4r ☎ 055 224 402 🖥 6, D

GALLERIA PONTE VECCHIO
Tucked away down a narrow alleyway off Via

OLTRARNO 🛍 **SHOPPING**

89

Guicciardini, this pretty little shop is full to the brim with brightly coloured Italian ceramics, which are guaranteed to cheer up your home.
🔢 E7 ✉ Via Guicciardini 104r ☎ 055 239 400 🚇 D

GIOVANNI TURCHI

This huge trove of period pieces is well worth delving into. The store has been in the family for many years, and has a huge amount of stock from the local area, Venice and the Veneto. Pieces are less expensive than they would be back home.
🔢 E7 ✉ Via Maggio 50–54r ☎ 055 217 341 🚇 D

GIULIO GIANNINI E FIGLIO

www.giuliogiannini.it
The best-known of Florence's stationery shops, established in 1856, sells tasteful cards and books bound in leather, as well as beautifully finished desktop paraphernalia, letter racks and pen holders, all covered with marbled paper.
🔢 E7 ✉ Piazza Pitti 37r ☎ 055 212 621 🚇 D

J. T. CASINI

www.casinifirenze.it
The latest in Italian and international designer clothing for women. Up-and-coming designers are showcased alongside well-known brands.
🔢 E7 ✉ Piazza Pitti 30–31r ☎ 055 219 324 🚇 D

MADOVA GLOVES

www.madova.com/shop
A staggering array of fine gloves lined with silk, cashmere and fur in every hue. Family run; established in 1919.
🔢 E7 ✉ Via Guicciardini 1r ☎ 055 239 6526 🚇 D

MOLERIA LOCCHI

www.locchi.com
This shop, next to the Prato dello Strozzino, sells the most extraordinary glass you will see outside Venice, created using authentic, traditional methods.
🔢 C7 ✉ Via Domenico Burchiello 10 ☎ 055 229 8371 🚇 D

OLIO & CONVIVIUM

www.conviviumfirenze.it
This pristine delicatessen ensures its first-class quality products respect

---

ARTISANS

The district of Oltrarno is characterized by small artisan workshops that tout their beautifully crafted objects, including textiles, ceramics, paper products and jewellery. Many of these businesses have been in the same family for generations and extreme skill and passion is employed in the workmanship. Every Monday and Thursday at 3pm, you can take a tour of three of these workshops (☎ 055 303 6108, or contact the tourist office; €10; no tours end July to mid-September).

---

local traditions. Bakery goods, cheeses, charcuterie and other fresh produce are beautifully displayed beside a huge range of olive oils and wine. There's an adjoining restaurant.
🔢 E6 ✉ Via Santo Spirito 4 ☎ 055 265 8198 🚇 11, D

PITTI BOUTIQUE

The wisdom and creativity of fine craftsmanship combine to make elegant and beautifully finished cashmere in brilliant and natural hues.
🔢 E7 ✉ Via dello Sprone 13r ☎ 055 280 285 🚇 11, D

RIVE GAUCHE

www.rivegaucheshoes.com
Many people visit Florence to buy the leather goods for which the city is renowned, in particular shoes. This shop takes you back in time with its beautiful handmade shoes and boots in Italian leather.
🔢 E7 ✉ Via Guicciardini 31r ☎ 055 213 474 🚇 D

IL TORCHIO

www.legatorioiltorchio.com
As you walk into this stationery shop you are instantly aware that this is a place where things are made, not just a showroom. You can buy sheets of marbled paper or have it made up to suit your requirements. There are also ready-made marbled paper goods available.
🔢 F7 ✉ Via dei Bardi 17 ☎ 055 234 2862 🚇 C, D

Entertainment and Nightlife

CAFFÈ RICCHI
This trendy Oltrarno bar is a good place to have coffee during the day, but it really only comes alive at night, especially in the summer, when you can sit outside.

➕ E7 ✉ Piazza Santo Spirito 9r ☎ 055 215 864 🕐 Closed Sun 🚌 11, D

CAVALLI CLUB
www.cavalliclub.com
Seeing is believing here, with typical Cavalli-style opulence and the inevitable animal prints throughout. Upstairs there is a restaurant, downstairs a stunning bar with a dance floor lowered after midnight. Opens at 7pm every night.

➕ D6 ✉ Piazza del Carmine 8r ☎ 055 211 650 🚌 D

LA DOLCE VITA
www.dolcevitaflorence.com
This is one of the hippest places for young Florentines to hang out. A great place for an *aperitivo* and to mingle with the preclub *bella gente*. It stays open until 2am.

➕ D6 ✉ Piazza del Carmine 6r ☎ 055 284 595 🚌 6, D

HEMINGWAY
www.hemingway.fi.it
Chic, funky café/bar serving light meals, great cocktails, speciality teas, fine coffees and chocolates, just off Piazza del Carmine. Stays open until 2am on Friday and Saturday.

➕ D6 ✉ Piazza Piattellina 9r ☎ 055 284 781 🚌 6, D

UNIVERSALE
www.universalefirenze.it
This former cinema space is now dedicated to dance music, cocktail drinking and Italian food. Mid-week focusses on commercial house while Saturday night sees a more eclectic music policy—funk, jazz and exotica.

➕ C6 ✉ Via Pisana 77r ☎ 055 221 122 🕐 Closed Mon, Tue, Wed 🚌 6, 12

Restaurants

AL TRANVAI (€)
www.altranvai.it
Diners are packed into this lively trattoria on the same square as the weekly market. Popular (with locals) is *frattaglie* (a mind-boggling range of offal) but the menu changes every day.

➕ C7 ✉ Piazza Torquato Tasso 14r ☎ 055 225 197 🕐 Closed Sun 🚌 12, 13

CAFFÈ PITTI (€–€€)
www.caffepitti.it
Just the place for a break in a perfect setting opposite the Palazzo Pitti. You can have breakfast, light lunch, tea or coffee any time. Have a predinner cocktail then a pleasant meal viewing the flood-lighted palazzo. Speciality of the house are the hand-picked unique truffles from the natural reserve owned by the Caffè Pitti, used to create some special dishes.

➕ E7 ✉ Piazza Pitti 9 ☎ 055 239 9863 🚌 D

CAMMILLO (€€–€€€)
A well-established trattoria that attracts an international crowd and a host of

Italian celebrities, enticed by the home-made pasta, various *baccalà* (salted cod) dishes and expertly cooked meats. Try some of the Masiero family's virgin olive oil with bread. Great choice of Tuscan and Piedmontese wines.

🔢 E6 ⊠ Borgo San Jacopo 57r ☎ 055 212 427 🕐 Closed Wed 🍽 D

IL CANTINONE (€–€€)

www.ilcantinonedifirenze.it
This restaurant is in an arched cellar. Long communal tables add a party atmosphere. Good wholesome fare.

🔢 E7 ⊠ Via de San Spirito 6r ☎ 055 218 898 🕐 Closed Mon 🍽 D

LA CASALINGA (€–€€)

A busy family-run place that is a good place to try *ribollita*, the Florentine soup made with bread and vegetables.

🔢 B8 ⊠ Via dei Michelozzi 9r ☎ 055 218 624 🕐 Closed Sun 🍽 D

MARACANA GRILL (€€)

www.maracanagrill.com
For something completely different, just steps away from the Piazza Santo Spirito, try this restaurant dedicated to the flavours of Brazil. The decor is bright and fun and the food spot on, particularly for carnivores.

🔢 E7 ⊠ Borgo Tegolaio 17r ☎ 055 238 2290 🕐 Closed Mon 🍽 D

OSTERIA DEL CINGHIALE BIANCO (€€)

www.cinghialebianco.it
The White Boar is named after one of Tuscany's greatest culinary specialities. Don't worry, there are chicken, veal and rabbit dishes as well.

🔢 E6 ⊠ Borgo San Jacopo 43r ☎ 055 215 706 🕐 Closed Wed dinner 🍽 11, D

OSTERIA SANTO SPIRITO (€€)

A delightful trattoria with outdoor seating and a menu of robust main courses and pasta dishes

---

CONTRADICTION

The concept of vegetarianism is not one that sits easily with Italian ideas about food, and there are very few vegetarian restaurants in Italy. However, there are few better countries for those who do not eat meat (or fish). Many pasta dishes contain no meat—pesto, tomato sauce or ravioli stuffed with spinach and ricotta, to name but a few. For a main course, try *grigliata di verdura* (grilled vegetables) or else restaurant stalwarts such as *parmigiana di melanzane* (aubergine [eggplant] layered with tomato and mozzarella, and baked with a Parmesan crust), *mozzarella in carrozza* (fried mozzarella) and *fritate* (omelettes).

---

such as oven-baked gnocchi in cheese and flavoured with truffles. Good for vegetarians and great for kids, too.

🔢 E7 ⊠ Piazza Santo Spirito 16r ☎ 055 238 2383 🍽 11, D

RISTORANTE BECCOFINO (€€)

www.beccofino.com
Chic, modern restaurant and wine bar. Experience Tuscan cooking with a twist—the chef worked in New York. In summer there is a terrace overlooking the river. Good wine list.

🔢 E6 ⊠ Piazza degli Scarlatti 1r ☎ 055 290 076 🍽 6, 11, D

TRATTORIA SANT'AGOSTINO 23 (€€)

www.sa23.it
This trattoria has a modern spin, with brightly coloured art on the walls. Mainly Tuscan cuisine is served although you'll find international dishes on the menu as well.

🔢 D7 ⊠ Via Sant'Agostino 23r ☎ 055 210 208 🕐 Closed Mon 🍽 11, D

LE VOLPI E L'UVA (€)

www.levolpieluva.com
A good little wine bar behind the Ponte Vecchio where you can wash down pungent Italian salamis and cheeses with robust Tuscan wines.

🔢 F7 ⊠ Piazza dei Rossi 1r ☎ 055 239 8132 🕐 Closed Sun 🍽 C3, D

Further Afield

There is plenty to do to escape the crowds or to have a change of scenery. Choose from pretty Fiesole, only 7km (4 miles) away; try medieval Siena and Lucca, or the Leaning Tower of Pisa, providing an irresistible pull.

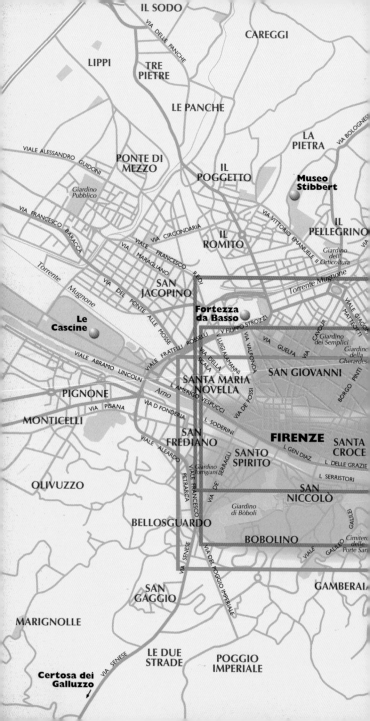

Typical Tuscan countryside (left); Fiesole's amphitheatre (below) and bell tower (right)

Fiesole

Perched on a hillside 7km (4 miles) above Florence, this delightful Etruscan-Roman town offers outstanding views over the city and the chance to visit an impressive archaeological complex, complete with amphitheatre, baths and a temple.

Take a stroll Fiesole provides the perfect antidote to hectic sightseeing in central Florence, while the bus ride there, climbing the winding road, is a pleasing introduction to the Tuscan countryside. Head first to the tourist information office to pick up a town map, which includes three walking routes that take in the best spots for views.

The archaeological area The entrance ticket to Fiesole's important Roman and Etruscan remains includes the Museo Civico and the small Museo Bandini. Set on a hillside, the open-air site features an Etruscan temple, the superbly preserved first-century AD Roman amphitheatre and the partially restored Roman baths. The theatre, holding 3,000 people, is still used today for performances and concerts during the Fiesole Summer Festival (▷ 103). On Vía Dupré, Museo Bandini houses 13th- to 15th-century Florentine paintings and Luca della Robbia terracottas.

Around the town Landmarks include the Duomo, with its 13th-century bell tower, and the striking 14th-century Palazzo Communale, now occupied by the town council. Several traditional restaurants and cafés overlook the main square.

THE BASICS

☐ Off map at M1
☒ Via Portigiani 3–5
☎ 055 596 1323
🕐 Mon–Fri 10–4.30, Sun and public hols 10–4
🚌 7
♿ Good
🎫 Combined ticket expensive

HIGHLIGHTS

● Views over Florence
● Archaeological area
● Roman amphitheatre
● Walks in the Tuscan countryside

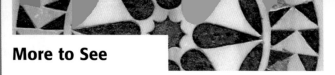

More to See

LE CASCINE

Florence's largest park was laid out by Napoleon's sister, Elisa Baciocchi Bonaparte, in 1811, on the site of the Medici dairy pastures (*cascine*). Every Tuesday there is a market, and there is also an open-air swimming pool in the park. The park is a long way from the heart of town and seedy by night.

➕ A3 ✉ Ponte della Vittoria 🕐 Daily 24 hours 🚌 17, 18 ♿ Good 🎟 Free

CERTOSA DI GALLUZZO

This great Carthusian monastery was once occupied by 18 monks, who lived silent lives. The stunning Chiostro Grande is decorated with *tondi* (circular works of art) by brothers Andrea and Giovanni della Robbia. The visit includes the Palazzo degli Studi, which holds great *Scenes from the Passion* frescoes, executed by Pontormo while he was sheltered here during the 1522 plague.

➕ Off map at C9 ✉ Certosa di Galluzzo, Via Buca di Certose 2 ☎ 055 204 9226 🕐 Tue– Sat 9.15–11.15, 3–5 🚌 37 ♿ Good 🎟 Free or donation ❓ Guided tours only

FORTEZZA DA BASSO

An enormous defensive fortress built in 1534 by Antonio da Sangallo il Giovane to the orders of Alessandro de' Medici. Today cars and buses hurtle around all sides, while the citadel hosts events and exhibitions.

➕ E3 ✉ Viale Filippo Strozzi ☎ Contact tourist office for events 🚌 4, 12, 13, 14, 20, 23

MUSEO STIBBERT

www.museostibbert.it

This bizarre museum, with superb armour, makes a fascinating diversion. The collection was amassed by Frederick Stibbert (1838–1906), who travelled the world, purchasing armour, porcelain, paintings, costume and much more. The museum is also worth visiting for its wooded grounds, complete with an Egyptian-style folly.

➕ Off map at F1 ✉ Via Frederico Stibbert 26 ☎ 055 475 520; 055 486 049 🕐 Mon– Wed 10–2, Fri–Sun 10–6 (last admission 1 hour before closing) 🚌 4 to Via Vittorio Emanuele II and steep 5-min walk to museum ♿ Most parts have access 🎟 Moderate ❓ Café and bookshop

Il Gioco del Ponte, *painted in the 17th century, is on display in Museo Stibbert*

Excursions

LUCCA

A prosperous town entirely enclosed within superb Renaissance walls with a rich heritage of churches and palaces.

The best starting point is Piazza Napoleone, with all the main sights only a few minutes' walk away. Begin at the Duomo, and its Museo della Cattedrale, then cross the square to Santi Giovanni e Reparata. Via Fillungo is an expensive shopping street that leads north to the Piazza Anfiteatro and San Frediano, another outstanding church. The main museums lie inside the walls to the west and east of the heart of town. Walking around the walls gives a fine overview of the town.

There are also spectacular views of the countryside farther afield from the 4km-long (2.5-mile) walls; you can see the distant Apuan Alps, which are covered in snow in winter.

THE BASICS

www.luccaturismo.it
Distance: 50km (31 miles)
Journey Time: About 1 hour
🚆 Regular departures from Santa Maria Novella station to Lucca Centrale
🛈 Piazza Santa Maria 35, Porto San Donato, Pizzzale Verdi
☎ 0583 919 931

PISA

The main draw is the architecture of the Campo dei Miracoli (Field of Miracles), home to the famous Leaning Tower.

The tower, reopened in 2001 after years of work to steady the tilt, stands next to the Romanesque-Gothic Duomo and Baptistery, the largest in Italy. All three buildings date from the 11th and 12th centuries, at the height of Pisa's power.

There is, however, more to Pisa than just its tower. The city is home to some 87,500 residents and there are more than 20 churches, several palaces and historic bridges to be explored. The pleasant cobbled streets of the shopping centre are a good place to stroll and find a café or restaurant. Check out the markets and mingle with the locals away from the tourist area around the tower. The daily food market (7–1.30) held in Piazza delle Vettovaglie, just off Borgo Stretto, is particularly lively.

THE BASICS

www.pisaunicaterra.it
Distance: 80km (50 miles)
Journey Time: 1 hour
🚆 Regular departures from Santa Maria Novella station to Pisa Centrale Station
🛈 Piazza Vittorio Emanuele II 16 (outside station)
☎ 050 42291

FURTHER AFIELD

EXCURSIONS

www.terresiena.it
Distance: 66km (41 miles)
Journey Time: 1–2 hours
🚆 Regular departures from Santa Maria Novella station
🚌 Rapide Sita bus leaves the Florence bus station to San Domenico in Sienna
ℹ️ Piazza del Campo 56
☎ 0577 280 551

SIENA

One of the loveliest towns in Italy, with great museums, interesting shops and many hills.

The focal point is fan-shaped Piazza del Campo, which slopes down to the bell tower. The Gothic cathedral was built between 1136 and 1382. Outside is a vast unfinished nave, begun in 1339 with the intention of making this the world's largest cathedral. Work was abandoned during the plague of 1348. Siena is home to the famous Palio, a horse race held in Piazza del Campo on 2 July and 16 August. Tickets for the event sell out months in advance; it is possible to stand but it does get very crowded and can be very hot. For a sense of Siena's size and layout, get a bird's-eye view by climbing the Torre del Mangia or the old cathedral wall. The historic centre of the city is closed to traffic making it easy for pedestrians, and fortunately all the main sights are in close proximity and easily walkable.

www.sangimignano.com
Distance: 57km (35 miles)
Journey Time: 1 hour
Route: Take the Firenze/ Siena *raccordo* (a motor-way link road) until the Poggibonsi exit. Follow the signs from here to San Gimignano—around 6km (4 miles)
Museo Leonardiano
✉️ Castello dei Conti Guidi, Vinci
☎ 0571 933251
🕐 Mar–Oct daily 9.30–7; Nov–Feb 9.30–6
🎟️ Moderate

TUSCAN COUNTRYSIDE

A country drive is a real treat. Much-visited San Gimignano is a prime destination with its hilltop site and medieval towers.

San Gimignano is the archetypical Tuscan town, perched on a hilltop and surrounded by vine-yards, olive groves and cypress trees. The towers of the medieval town can be seen from some distance away. Only 15 of the original 72 towers remain, but their impact is still breathtaking. There are several museums to visit and particular products to buy, including San Gimignano wine and olive oil. For pots, stop in Montelupo, where many of Florence's ceramics have been made for centuries. On your way back visit Vinci, the birthplace of Leonardo da Vinci with a museum about his life. If you want a swim, the village of Sambuca, near Tavarnelle, has an outdoor pool. Deep in the countryside you can find olives and wine for sale.

Shopping

Lucca

CANIPAROLI

This shop is a choco-holic's heaven. Chunks of chocolate adorn the window, along with calorific but divine cakes, such as the naughty but delicious *Sachertorte*.

✉ Via Paolino 96 ☎ 0583 53456 🕐 Tue–Sat 9.30–1, 3.30–7.30

CERAMICHE DI SUGARÒ

The highly decorative traditional ceramics in this shop conjour up the warm tones of the Tuscan countryside. Everything for the table from huge platters to delightful egg cups in the shape of a chicken. Your goods can be shipped home.

✉ Piazza Napoleone 17 ☎ 0583 464 557 🕐 Closed Mon am

CERAMISTI D'ARTÉ

www.ceramistidarte.it
Tuscan artists Stefano Seardo and Fabrizio Falchi sculpt and paint at this workshop. Visit to pick up hand-painted decorative tiles, terracotta sculptures and marble mosaics. Everything is produced according to ancient Italian ceramic techniques.

✉ Via Santa Gemma Galgani 1 ☎ 0583 467 224 🕐 Tue–Sun 9.30–1, 3.30–8, Mon 3.30–7.30

MARSILI COSTANTINO

Marsali gives a tasty introduction to Lucca's local vineyards, with some lesser-known but delicious wines. Also try some of the herb liqueurs and *digestifs* that are produced using local recipes.

✉ Piazza San Michele 38 ☎ 0583 491 751 🕐 Jun–Sep daily 9–7.30; Oct–May Tue–Sat 9–1, 3.30–7.30, Mon 3.30–7.30

TADDEUCCI

www.buccellatotaddeucci.com
This shop, founded by Jacopo Taddeucci in 1881, is in Lucca's main square. It is renowned for the *buccellato*, a sweet ring-shape cake made with raisins and flavoured with anise. There are also plenty more tempting cakes and patisserie to choose from, together with sweets and chocolates.

✉ Piazza San Michele 34 ☎ 0583 494 933 🕐 Daily 8.30–8 (closed Thu Nov–Feb)

Pisa

BACCHUS ENOTECA

www.bacchusenoteca.com
Just a short distance from the main train station, this specialist wine shop is the perfect place to buy the best of Tuscan wines. You will also find spirits and liqueurs, as well as sweets, oils and other delicacies.

✉ Via Mascagni 1 ☎ 050 500 560 🕐 Tue–Sun 9–1, 4–8

FEDERICO SALZA

www.salza.it
An outlet of the popular Turin confectioner sells beautifully fashioned chocolates and pastries. Look for the chocolate Leaning Tower of Pisa.

✉ Borgo Stretto 46 ☎ 050 580 144 🕐 Jun–Oct daily 8–8.30; Nov–May Tue–Sun 8–8.30

LENZI GHINO GIACOMO

www.ceramichelenzi.it
This factory shop, to the west of Pisa toward Vicopisano, sells classic Tuscan ceramics and its owners pride themselves on producing basins, vases and pottery the traditional way. Choose from vases and crockery splashed with green and white—the beautifully decorated pots for storing oil, wine and herbs make great gifts.

✉ Via Provinciale Vicarese 371, San Giovanni alla Vena ☎ 050 799 015 🕐 Mon–Sat 9–1, 3–8

Siena

ANTICHITÀ MONNA AGNESE

One of Siena's better antiques stores, stocking furniture and silver as well as other items. There is another, smaller shop on the opposite side of the street, which deals in antique jewellery.

✉ Via di Città 45 and 60
☎ 0577 282 288

CERAMICHE ARTISTICHE SANTA CATERINA

A family business run by the founder, Marcello Neri, his wife and son. The whole family works in the traditional Sienese styles of ceramics using only black, white and *terra di Siena*, or burnt siena glass glazes. Their designs are inspired by local architecture, especially the Duomo, and you can watch them at work.

✉ Via di Città 74
☎ 0577 283 098

CORTECCI ABBIGLIAMENTO

www.corteccisiena.it
In business since 1935, this shop's large collection of men's and women's designer labels includes Gucci, Armani, Yves Saint Laurent, Christian Dior, Roberto Cavalli and Dolce & Gabbana. There are two branches of this shop and this one has the more classic collections, while the other branch

at Il Campo 30, stocks labels aimed at a younger market.

✉ Via Banchi di Sopra 27
☎ 0577 280 096

DROGHERIA MANGANELLI

A must for foodies. The shop is a member of the Slow Food Movement, an organization that promotes organic food, grown and cooked using traditional methods. It has been selling local produce since 1879, with an array of cured meats and fine farmhouse cheeses, as well as vinegars, wine and the best virgin olive oils. Try the *ricciarelli* (almond cookies), traditionally served with sweet wine and enjoyed year-round.

MARKETS

There are daily food markets in provincial and regional capitals and other large towns. They generally take place in a purpose-built market hall or in a specific square or street, selling meat, groceries, fish, dairy products, fruit and vegetables. Where there's a daily food market, the weekly market will be devoted to everything else from clothes and shoes to household goods, plants and fabrics. In Florence the most prominent are Mercato Centrale (▷ 68), Mercato di Sant'Ambrogio (▷ 38) and Mercato Nuovo (▷ 37).

✉ Via di Città 71–73
☎ 0577 205 000

MORBIDI

One of the best-known Sienese delicatessens, selling Tuscan salamis and the more unusual *finochiona* (salami made from fennel). Be sure to try the local cheeses, such as *pecorino* or the oval-shaped *fresco di Monnalisa*, and pâtés that are great for picnics.

✉ Via Banchi di Sopra 75
☎ 0577 280 268

SIENA RICAMA

This embroidery and needlework shop is run by Signora Fontani, who makes all the goods herself. Drawing inspiration from medieval designs, local art, frescoes and manuscripts, the beautifully embroidered or cross-stitched items include clothing, soft furnishings, lampshades and tapestries.

✉ Via di Città 61
☎ 0577 288 339

TESSUTI A MANO

Drop into this workshop and boutique to pick up beautiful, hand-woven accessories and fashionable garments. Designer Fioretta Bacci can often be seen sitting at a loom weaving her much sought-after scarves, shawls and items of clothing.

✉ Via San Pietro 7
☎ 0577 282 200

Entertainment and Nightlife

AUDITORIUM FLOG
www.flog.it
This is probably the best known of Florence's live music venues, where music of all kinds is played; regular themed disco evenings.
🔢 Off map 📧 Via Mercati 24b ☎ 055 477 978 🚌 4

CENTRAL PARK
This complex has a garden, eight bars, four dance floors, a restaurant and VIP terrace. Italian house dominates but there's also plenty of room for loungecore and smooth piano-bar music.
🔢 B4 📧 Via del Fosso Macinate 2, Parco delle Cascine ☎ 055 359 942
🕐 Closed Mon 🚌 1, 9, 12

ESTATE FIESOLANA
A season of music, opera and ballet known as the Sunset Concerts, primarily in Fiesole's open-air Teatro Romano (▷ 97), from late June to September. Reserve in advance and then head for the Fiesole hills, above the city. The concerts are an unbeatable experience.
Estate Fiesolana
🔢 Off map ☎ Contact APT (tourist information), Fiesole 055 596 1323
Teatro Romano
🔢 Off map 📧 Via Marini 🚌 7

GIRASOL
www.girasol.it
Florentines have a passion for Latin American bars. This is the best, with live and recorded Cuban, Caribbean and other Latin-American music.
🔢 D1 📧 Via del Romito 1r ☎ 055 474 948 🚌 14

NELSON MANDELA FORUM
www.mandelaforum.it
This medium-size venue near Campo Marte hosts some of Italy's most celebrated rock and pop acts. Check in advance for British and US bands who may be playing here.
🔢 M4 📧 Viale P Paoli 3 ☎ Box office Via Alamanini 055 678 841 for tickets
🚌 3, 10

PALAZZO DEI CONGRESSI
This palazzo hosts many conferences and cultural events throughout the year. Look out for the occasional choral and classical concerts held in one of the fine salons.

MAGGIO MUSICALE FIORENTINO

This major musical festival held in May and June includes opera and ballet as well as orchestral concerts and chamber music. It has its own orchestra, chorus and ballet troupe. The main venue is the Teatro Comunale; the Teatro della Pergola and the Teatro Verdi are used for more intimate recitals. The main box office is at the Teatro Comunale.

🔢 E3 📧 Viale Filippo Strozzi ☎ Box office Via Alamanini 055 210 804 for tickets; check with tourist office for events 🚌 6, 11, 22, 36, 37, A

PINOCCHIO JAZZ
www.pinocchiojazz.it
Some of Italy's top jazz artists play here during the two-season agenda. Members nod approvingly in this smoky venue while musicians play into the night. Check *Firenze Spettacolo* for what's on.
🔢 M8 📧 Viale Giannotti 13 ☎ 055 683 388 🚌 31, 32

MECCANO
This large, popular club caters for a wide range of tastes including mainstream, house and funk. Aimed primarily at a young crowd, it's like a big house party on several floors. A chance to let your hair down.
🔢 B4 📧 Via degli Olmi, Parco delle Cascine ☎ 055 331 371 🕐 Closed Mon, Sun 🚌 1, 9

TENAX
www.tenax.org
Trendy and up-to-date music and a huge dance floor; very popular with both Florentines and foreigners. As a superclub, it has some mind-blowing lighting and sound technology and some very curious art installations. Also hosts various live music acts.
🔢 Off map 📧 Via Pratese 46 ☎ 055 308 160 🕐 Check schedule 🚌 29, 30

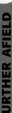

Sport

CANOTTIERI COMUNALI FIRENZE

www.canottiericomunali
firenze.it

Have a go at boating, rowing or canoeing at this club on the River Arno. Courses are available.

➕ L7 ✉ Lungarno Ferrucci 2 ☎ 055 681 2151 🚍 3, 8, 31, 32, 80

CIRCOLO DEL GOLF DELL'UGOLINO

www.golfugolino.it

Founded in 1933, this 18-hole, 72-par attractive course has hosted many famous golfing greats.

➕ Off map to south ✉ Via Chiantigiana 3, Grassina (10km/6miles south on road to Siena) ☎ 055 230 1009

CLUB SPORTIVO FIRENZE TENNIS

www.clubsportivofirenze.it

Situated in Le Cascine park (▷ 98); there are two clay courts (covered in winter) in pleasant surroundings.

➕ A4 ✉ Viale del Visarno 10 ☎ 055 332 701 🚍 1, 9, 12, 16, 26, 27, 80

GOLF CLUB MONTELUPO

www.golfmontelupo.it

This 3,067-yard, par 36, 9-hole golf course lies below the Chianti Montalbano hills on the banks of the Arno. Enjoy the scenery and excellent facilities, including a pro shop, practice area and putting greens. Coaching is available.

➕ Off map ✉ Fattoria di Fibbiana, Via le Piagge 4, Montelupo (19km/12 miles to west of Florence) ☎ 0571 541 004 🕐 Call for times

IPPODROMI FIORENTINI

The Ippodromo delle Mulina is the place to go and see horse racing in Florence (flat racing or trotting racing). Telephone or check the local press for meetings. In 2013, the future of the track was uncertain.

➕ B4 ✉ Le Cascine ☎ 055 422 591; trotting racing 055 422 59217 🚍 14

PAGANELLI

Open six days a week for swimming, there are also courses for adults and children, which include diving and aquagym.

FOOTBALL IS ALL

Many Florentines take more pride in their football (soccer) team than in their artistic heritage. Until 2002 AC Fiorentina, also known as the 'Viola' (the Purples), were one of the top clubs in Italy, but following a financial scandal the club was declared bankrupt and demoted three divisions. The team clawed its way back into Serie A and regained its former glory. Games take place at the Stadio Artemio Franchi, where you can join the ever-faithful fans cheering on the lads in lavender.

➕ Off map ✉ Viale Guidoni 208, Novoli ☎ 055 437 9787 🕐 Closed Tue 🚍 5, 22

PALESTRA TROPOS

www.troposfirenze.it

This well-established gym has classes for all ages, including aerobics and hydrobike exercises. Two swimming pools.

➕ K6 ✉ Via Orcagna 20a ☎ 055 678 381 🚍 14, 31, 32

PISCINA COMUNALE BELLARIVA

An outdoor Olympic swimming pool with a smaller one for children in pleasant shady gardens east of the city.

➕ M7 ✉ Lungarno A Moro ☎ 055 677 521 🕐 Jun–Sep 🚍 14

PISCINA LE PAVONIERE

Most popular and the prettiest outdoor swimming pool in Florence, in Le Cascine (▷ 98).

➕ A4 ✉ Viale della Catena 2 ☎ 055 321 5644 🕐 Jun–Sep 🚍 17

STADIO COMUNALE ARTEMIO FRANCHI

The Stadio Comunale Artemio Franchi or the Palazzo dello Sport, is where AC Fiorentina (▷ panel) play football (soccer) on alternate Sundays from September to May. Tickets are sold at the entrance and in cafés near by.

➕ L3 ✉ Campo di Marte, Viale Manfredo Fanti 4 ☎ 055 503 011 🚍 17

Restaurants

Fiesole

RISTORANTE IL FIESOLANO (PERSEUS) (€€)

This is one of Florence's best restaurants in which to sample the famous *bistecca alla fiorentina* (T-bone steak, ▷ panel). Other classic Tuscan dishes are served on a terrace facing the Teatro Romano in Fiesole.

🔝 Off map at M1 ✉ Piazza Mino da Fiesole 9 ☎ 055 591 43 🕐 Limited winter opening 🚌 7

RISTORANTE I POLPA (€€)

Eat at this friendly place and enjoy a magnificent night view over Florence. Not only is there an open wood-burning grill, but the oven is lighted, too, for cooking *crostini*—toasted crusty bread with a variety of tasty toppings.

🔝 Off map at M1 ✉ Piazza Mino da Fiesole 21–22 ☎ 055 50485 🕐 Thu–Tue 7–10 🚌 7

RISTORANTE LA LOGGIA SAN MICHELE (€€€)

www.villasanmichele.com
The evocative former monastery setting and some of the finest cuisine in the area attract diners to this Fiesole restaurant, to be found in the hotel Villa San Michele (▷ 112).

🔝 Off map at M1 ✉ Via Doccia 4 ☎ 055 567 8200 🕐 Daily lunch and dinner; closed end Nov to end Mar 🚌 7

Lucca

BUCA DI SANT ANTONIO (€€)

www.bucadisantantonio.com
One of the oldest, as well as the most popular, restaurants in Lucca. The menu is all à la carte, with an emphasis on Lucchese cuisine, and the use of seasonal, freshly produced ingredients.

✉ Via della Cervia 3 ☎ 0583 55881 🕐 Tue–Sat lunch and dinner, Sun lunch

NATURALLY ROBUST

The classic Florentine dish is *bistecca alla fiorentina* (T-bone steak sold by the weight, usually 100g). Grilled and served rare with lemon wedges, it can be found on the menu in the majority of Florentine restaurants. Other traditional dishes include *trippa alla fiorentina* (tripe stewed with tomatoes and served with Parmesan), *crostini* (toasted bread with a variety of toppings), and *panzanella* (a salad of crumbled bread tossed with tomatoes with olive oil, onions, basil and parsley).

OSTERIA MACHIAVELLI (€–€€)

Small trattoria a few paces from Piazza San Salvatore in the middle of Lucca. Predominantly Tuscan and Lucchese cuisine with the usual mixture of cold cuts, a range of interesting sausages, grilled meats, roasts and home-made pastas. The small but well-chosen wine list complements the cooking.

✉ Via C Battisti 28 ☎ 0583 467 219 🕐 Mon–Sat lunch and dinner

ROUSSEAU IL DOGANIERE (€–€€)

Full of character, this restaurant and pizzeria serves good fresh home-made pasta, beef dishes sourced from local cattle, fish, soup and excellent pizza from the traditional firewood oven. Outdoor seating in summer.

✉ Via Vittorio Emanuele II 28 ☎ 0583 584 214 🕐 Wed–Mon lunch and dinner

TRATTORIA DA LEO (€)

www.trattoriadaleo.it
Popular family-run trattoria where you can eat in the dining room, with its pastel walls and wooden furnishings, or on the simple but shaded terrace. The owners make you feel at home, sometimes sitting and chatting after the meal.

✉ Via Tegrimi 1 ☎ 0583 492 236 🕐 Daily lunch and dinner

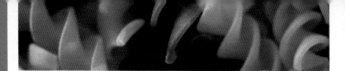

Pisa

LA BUCA (€–€€)

www.labuca.org

In a popular spot in the heart of Pisa, Buca draws the crowds to its pleasant terrace and the set-price lunch menu, which offers Tuscan cuisine at a reasonable price. Dinner is little more formal but still with lots of pizza and pasta choices.

✉ Via G Tassi 6/B ☎ 050 560 660 🕐 Sat–Thu lunch and dinner

DA BRUNO (€€–€€€)

www.anticatrattoriadabruno.com

Self-proclaimed as the best restaurant in Pisa, this long-established trattoria serves traditional local cuisine. The two dining rooms have wood-beamed ceilings, long, elegant tables, and white-washed walls covered with photographs of the famous people who have dined here under patron Piero Cei's watchful eye. Reserve in advance.

✉ Via Luigi Bianchi 12 ☎ 050 560 818 🕐 Thu–Mon lunch and dinner, Wed dinner

Siena

AL MARSILI (€€–€€€)

Not far from the cathedral, this is one of Siena's classiest restaurants where you can try Sienese cuisine in an attractive vaulted dining room. The menu includes both traditional dishes and some more creative takes on the local cuisine. Sample one of their most famous dishes, the *faraona alla Medici* (meaty guinea fowl cooked with pine nuts, almonds and prunes) or the tasty lemon risotto.

✉ Via del Castoro 3 ☎ 0577 47154 🕐 Tue–Sun lunch and dinner

IL CAMPO (€–€€)

This is the original restaurant on the Piazza del Campo and a great spot for people-watching. A consequence of this is that service may suffer at busy times. The menu is a mix of Italian and European cusine. They don't take reservations.

✉ Piazza del Campo 50–51 ☎ 0577 280 725

ICE CREAM

Italian ice cream—*gelato*—is generally of very high quality. Italians would rather pay more and eat something made with fresh ingredients. So a basic ice cream is usually made with milk, cream, eggs and sugar, and the tastes are strikingly pure and direct. A popular choice is *crema*—egg custard—good with a scoop of intense dark chocolate or pungent coffee. People usually opt for a selection of *creme* or *frutte* (creams or fruit) and don't mix the two types. The best *gelaterie* serve fruit varieties made from whatever fruits are in season.

🕐 Wed–Mon lunch and dinner

OSTERIA LE LOGGE (€€–€€€)

www.giannibrunelli.it

In a former medieval pharmacy, this charming restaurant is just off the Campo. There are tables outside, plus two dining areas. The menu is full of classic Tuscan dishes. Reservations are advised.

✉ Via del Porrione 33 ☎ 0577 48013 🕐 Mon–Sat lunch and dinner

SOTTO LE FONTI (€€)

www.sottolefonti.it

This medieval building has been beautifully renovated to recreate an old-fashioned restaurant. The menu is based on Sienese dishes, such as salami, game, or lamb chops with juniper. The scrumptious cakes and desserts are all home-made.

✉ Via Esterna Fontebranda 14 ☎ 0577 226 446 🕐 Daily lunch and dinner

LA TAVERNA DI SAN GIUSEPPE (€–€€)

www.tavernasangiuseppe.it

This lively trattoria specializes in Tuscan food, with an emphasis on meat, although vegetarians are well catered to with a rich vegetable soup, *ribollita*. Intimate cellar-like dining room.

✉ Via Giovanni Duprè 132 ☎ 0577 42286 🕐 Mon–Sat lunch and dinner; closed last 2 weeks in Jan and Jul

Florence is one of Italy's top destinations and hotels are, on the whole, expensive. Check out the internet before leaving home to catch some seasonal deals. Staying out of season is your best bet.

Introduction

Choose from world-class hotels in historic buildings, ultrachic boutique hotels or family-run *pensiones* that haven't changed much in 30 years. Houses and apartments offering bed and breakfast are an option that is becoming very popular.

Hotels

Tuscan hotels (*alberghi*) are graded by the regional authorities on a star rating of one to five. These refer to the facilities provided rather than character or comfort. Expect five-star hotels to be grand, with superb facilities and service; four-star establishments will be almost as good. Three-star hotels are more idiosyncratic. Prices can vary enormously, as can the public areas and staffing levels; but all rooms will have a television and telephone. One and two stars are relatively inexpensive, clean and comfortable, and rooms almost always have private bathrooms in two-star places. Breakfast is usually included, although often poor.

Pensiones

There's little difference between simpler hotels and *pensiones*; both are usually family-run, and provide spotlessly clean, comfortable rooms at a fair price. Some *pensiones* may be a little dated, but this is also the case in smaller hotels.

Rooms to Rent

Signs saying rooms (*camere* or *zimmer*) are rooms to rent in private houses and are a good option if money is tight or you can't find a hotel. Local tourist offices keep a list.

RESERVATIONS

Florence is so popular that you will need to book in advance at whatever time of year you decide to visit. If you're booking in advance from home, make certain you get written confirmation and take it with you. Without this, you may turn up and find all knowledge of your booking denied. If you make an internet booking, print out your booking confirmation and take it with you.

You will appreciate somewhere comfortable to relax and unwind after your journey or a day sightseeing

Budget Hotels

PRICES

Expect to pay up to €100 per night for a double room in a budget hotel

ALBERGO FIRENZE

www.hotelfirenze-fi.it

A 57-room modern hotel in a very quiet courtyard in the heart of Florence.

➕ F6 ✉ Piazza dei Donati 4
☎ 055 268 301 🚌 C2

BRETAGNA

www.hotelbretagna.net

Eighteen affordable rooms with views of the River Arno.

➕ E6 ✉ Lungarno Corsini 6
☎ 055 289 618 🚌 C3

CHIAZZA

www.chiazzahotel.com

In the Santa Croce area, this hotel offers a smart, comfortable budget option. Not far from the Duomo, some of the 14 rooms look out onto the terracotta-tiled rooftops.

➕ H5 ✉ Borgo Piniti 5
☎ 055 248 0363 🚌 C1, C3

CRISTINA

www.hotelcristina-florence.com

A small, friendly hotel in a medieval palace off a quiet street in the heart of Florence. The nine rooms (four en suite) have high ceilings and wood furniture. It's good value and the delightful owners make it perfect for families. Because of this, it is a popular choice so make reservations well ahead.

➕ F6 ✉ Via della Condotta 4 ☎ 055 214 484 🚌 C2

JOHANNA I

www.johanna.it

Beautifully renovated, the 11 rooms are small but beautifully furnished and there is an intimate communal room with a fridge.

➕ G3 ✉ Via Bonifacio Lupi 14 ☎ 055 481 896 🚌 C2

NUOVA ITALIA

www.hotel-nuovaitalia.com

Modern, clean 20-room hotel with friendly staff.

➕ E4 ✉ Via Faenza 26
☎ 055 287 508 🚌 T1

PALAZZO GUADAGNI

www.palazzoguadagni.com

Set in a quiet area in the Oltrarno, this lovely hotel retains all the architectural elements associated with the best of Tuscan style—huge fireplaces, frescoed ceilings and oak beams. Factor in modern amenities, antique furniture and some of the loveliest views in the

CAMPING

Campeggio Michelangelo, on the hills south of the Arno, is just a short bus ride from central Florence. It has hot showers, toilets, washing machines, electricity points, internet access, a supermarket and a bar that looks out over the city. There are 240 pitches. Open all year

➕ H8 ✉ Viale Michelangelo 80 ☎ 055 681 1977; www.ecvacanze.it

🚌 12, 13

city and you have a great place to stay. There is a fabulous view from the rooftop loggia bar.

➕ E7 ✉ Piazza Santo Spirito 9 ☎ 055 265 8376
🚌 D

PENSIONE MARIA LUISA DE' MEDICI

Characterful 17th-century house cluttered with objects d'art. The nine rooms vary in size—some are very large and two have a private bathroom. Excellent value with breakfast included, and situated very close to the Duomo. Not for night owls as the owner imposes a curfew (time varies with season).

➕ F5 ✉ Via del Corso 1
☎ 055 280 048 🚌 C2

SCOTI

www.hotelscoti.com

Atmospheric 15th-century building in an excellent location directly opposite the Palazzo Strozzi, in the shopping mecca of Via de' Tornabuoni. It's a great place to stay—excellent value, with period character, and a good central base from which to explore the city. The 11 bedrooms are simple and light. There are no private bathrooms, but the shared ones are very clean. The lounge area has attractive 18th-century frescoes depicting Italian landscapes.

➕ E6 ✉ Via de' Tornabuoni 7 ☎ 055 292 128 🚌 C1, C2

Mid-Range Hotels

PRICES

Expect to pay between €100 and €250 per night for a double room in a mid-range hotel

ANNALENA

www.annalena.com
In a Medici palazzo opposite the Boboli Gardens, this hotel was once the haunt of artists and writers. Some of the 20 rooms have terraces and views. A lovely peaceful spot.
➕ D8 ✉ Via Romana 34 ☎ 055 222 402 🚌 36, 37, D

BALESTRI

www.hotel-balestri.it
Close to the River Arno, between the Uffizi and Santa Croce, with 51 comfortable rooms.
➕ F5 ✉ Piazza Mentana 7 ☎ 055 214 743
🚌 C3, D

BELLETTINI

www.hotelbellettini.com
Close to San Lorenzo and the Duomo, this hotel, with 28 rooms and 5 suites, dates from the 15th century, making it one of the oldest in Florence as well as one of the friendliest. Rooms come in a variety of sizes; optional private bathroom. Breakfast includes the owner's melt-in-the-mouth home baking and should not be missed.
➕ F5 ✉ Via de' Conti 7 ☎ 055 213 561 🚌 C1, C2

CASCI

www.hotelcasci.com
A family-run hotel, with 25 rooms, and once home to the Italian composer Gioacchino Rossini. Although modernized, it still has some of its original 14th-century features. Immaculate, functional rooms a short stroll from the Duomo.
➕ F4 ✉ Via Cavour 13 ☎ 055 211 686 🚌 C1

LE DUE FONTANE

www.leduefontane.it
Modern 57-room hotel in the delightful Piazza della Santissima Annunziata.
➕ G4 ✉ Piazza della Santissima Annunziata 14 ☎ 055 210 185 🚌 C1, C2

GALILEO

www.galileohotel.it
Bright and cheerful hotel ideal for those who want to make the most of every minute in Florence. The 31 rooms are clean and relaxing and have all the amenities you might require.

WHICH ROOM?

The room with a view is a much sought-after thing. However, it can often come with street noise. Most Florentine hotels are in palazzi built around courtyards, so the rooms with views face onto the street, while the ones looking over the courtyards are pleasantly quiet. You might prefer to forego the romance to ensure a good night's sleep.

➕ E4 ✉ Via Nazionale 22a ☎ 055 496 645 🚌 4, 25, 31

HERMITAGE

www.hermitagehotel.com
A well-known 29-room hotel overlooking the Ponte Vecchio that draws visitors back time and time again. Its light and airy roof garden is an idyllic place to relax after a day exploring the city.
➕ F6 ✉ Vicolo Marzio 1, Piazza del Pesce ☎ 055 287 216 🚌 C3, D

KRAFT

www.krafthotel.it
This hotel has been renovated to include energy-saving technology in the 80 comfortable rooms. There is a small rooftop swimming pool and some terrific views.
➕ C5 ✉ Via Solferino 2 ☎ 055 284 273 🚌 C1, C3, D

LOGGIATO DEI SERVITI

www.loggiatodeiservitihotel.it
You can relax under vaulted ceilings, amid dark-wood antiques and rich fabrics in the former monastery of the Serviti. The rooms are enlivened by bright curtains and throws. Many look onto the arcades of Piazza Santissima Annunziate. The 38 rooms have private bathrooms and the breakfast room has views of the Accademia gardens.
➕ G4 ✉ Piazza Santissima Annunziata 3 ☎ 055 289 592 🚌 C1, C2

MARIO'S
www.hotelmarios.com
This small family-run hotel is an example of the great value for money that can still be found in this expensive city. It feels as if you are staying in someone's home, with care and attention paid to the 16 atmospheric rooms and to your needs.
⊞ E4 ✉ Via Faenza 89
☎ 055 216 801 🚌 T1

PALAZZO RUSPOLI
www.palazzo-ruspoli.it
Ideally placed close to the Duomo and San Lorenzo, this 20-room hotel is an immaculate and comfortable place to stay with its attractive paintwork and patterned soft furnishings.
⊞ F5 ✉ Via de' Martelli 5
☎ 055 267 0563 🚌 C1, C2

LA RESIDENZA
www.laresidenzahotel.com
Comfortable 23-room hotel on the top four floors of a 17th-century palazzo on the super-elegant Via de' Tornabuoni. A complete overhaul has resulted in some exceptionally well-appointed rooms with huge bathrooms. Rooms at the top have balconies and there is a small roof terrace. Friendly and considerate owners ensure an enjoyable stay. Free internet access is available.
⊞ E6 ✉ Via de' Tornabuoni 8 ☎ 055 218 684 🚌 C2, C3

RIVOLI
www.hotelrivoli.it
Close to Santa Maria Novella, the Rivoli is a beautifully renovated Franciscan monastery. The 80 rooms are well furnished, with large marble bathrooms. Request one of the rooms with a balcony or terrace.
⊞ E5 ✉ Via della Scala 33
☎ 055 278 61 🚌 C2, D

LA SCALETTA
www.lascaletta.com
For those who want to stay on the quieter south side of the River Arno, La Scaletta is a good choice. The hotel is set in a peaceful spot close to Oltrarno and the Boboli Gardens. The 14 rooms have a welcoming, homey feel. There is a lovely rooftop terrace.
⊞ E7 ✉ Via de Guicciardini 13 ☎ 055 283 028 🚌 D

TORNABUONI BEACCI
www.tornabuonihotels.com
A handsome hotel that's well placed for shopping and sightseeing. The large, leafy roof garden and antiques-filled lounge are quiet retreats from the bustle outside on this busy street. The 28 bedrooms are simple and uncluttered, and each has its own private bathroom.
⊞ E6 ✉ Via de' Tornabuoni 3 ☎ 055 212 645 🚌 C2, C3

VILLA FIESOLE
www.villafiesole.it
In the hilltop village of Fiesole, this hotel with 32 rooms has an outdoor pool and a wonderful Victorian greenhouse that accommodates the breakfast room, a lounge area and several bed-rooms. This hotel offers really good value for great surroundings.
⊞ Off map at M1 ✉ Via Beato Angelico 35 ☎ 055 597 252 🚌 7

VILLANI
www.hotelvillani.it
Experience real value for the money at this 13-room hotel that attracts an interesting mix of visitors, including Italian families. It's situated conveniently close to the Duomo. There are great views from the top-floor terrace.
⊞ F5 ✉ Via delle Oche 11
☎ 055 239 6451 🚌 C2

Luxury Hotels

PRICES

Expect to pay over €250 per night for a double room in a luxury hotel

BRUNELLESCHI

www.hotelbrunelleschi.it
A modern 96-room hotel housed in a medieval tower in a peaceful location just behind the Via Calzaiuoli.
➕ F5 ✉ Piazza Santa Elisabetta 3 ☎ 055 273 370 🚌 C2

GRAND HOTEL VILLA MEDICI

www.villamedicihotel.com
A little way from the main attractions, this hotel is peaceful and has lovely gardens and a pool overlooked by the top-notch restaurant. Elegant public rooms, classy bedrooms and a fitness centre complete the picture.
➕ D4 ✉ Via Il Prato 42 ☎ 055 277 171 🚌 D

HELVETIA & BRISTOL

www.royaldemeure.com
An 18th-century hotel in a superb location near the Duomo. Each of the 34 rooms and 18 suites is decorated individually with rich furnishings, and some have antiques, too.
➕ E5 ✉ Via dei Pescioni 2 ☎ 055 266 51 🚌 C2

J. K. PLACE

www.jkplace.com
This small, chic hotel is a fabulous blend of old and new, where modern art is cleverly displayed alongside antique features. Oozing sophistication, the sleek bedrooms and homey day rooms are portrayed with attention to detail. There's a pleasant rooftop terrace.
➕ E5 ✉ Piazza Santa Maria Novella 7 ☎ 055 264 5181 🚌 All buses to Santa Maria Novella station

PALAZZO MAGNANI FERONI

www.palazzomagnaniferoni.it
This is a grand place to stay by the side of the River Arno. It has an inner courtyard, vaulted ceilings and lots of marble. There are 12 suites in all.
➕ D6 ✉ Borgo San Frediano 5 ☎ 055 239 9544 🚌 D

RIVA LOFTS FLORENCE

www.rivalofts.com
Superb hotel created from a former factory. Designed by architect Claudio Nardi, the eight fabulous studios offer park or river views. Around a 30-minute walk to central Florence.

LAST-MINUTE

If you arrive without a reservation, try the ITA (Informazioni Turistiche Alberghiere) office on the train station concourse (🕐 Daily 8–7.30 ☎ 055 282 893). You'll pay a fee of around €3–€8 for finding a room, depending on the category of hotel.

➕ Off map at A4 ✉ Via Baccio Bandinelli 98 ☎ 055 713 0272 🚌 No buses

ST. REGIS FLORENCE

www.stregisflorence.com
Sumptuous hotel in a 19th-century palazzo overlooking the River Arno with 107 gorgeously decorated rooms.
➕ D5 ✉ Piazza Ognissanti 1 ☎ 055 288 781 🚌 A, B

SAVOY

www.hotelsavoy.it
This 19th-century building in Piazza della Republicca is one of Florence's top boutique hotels. It has 88 sleek rooms and 14 suites.
➕ F5 ✉ Piazza della Republicca 7 ☎ 055 27351 🚌 C2

VILLA SAN MICHELE

www.villasanmichele.com
Nestling in the Fiesole hills high above Florence, this former monastery with 46 rooms offers the lushest of surroundings and the plushest of interiors. Superb views.
➕ Off map at M1 ✉ Via Doccia 4, Fiesole ☎ 055 567 8200 🚌 7

WESTIN EXCELSIOR

www.westinflorence.com
The Westin Excelsior is one of the grandest hotels in Florence, renowned for its opulence. Some of the 171 rooms have river views, and there is a roof terrace.
➕ D5 ✉ Piazza Ognissanti 3 ☎ 055 271 51 🚌 C3, D

Florence is compact and the public transportation good. Walking is probably one of the best and most rewarding ways of getting around. Petty crime is common but the city is relatively safe.

Planning Ahead

When to Go

Florence's peak season runs from March to October, although many consider it virtually uninterrupted. The city is overrun with tour groups in June and July. If you like heat, go in August—although many Florentines are on holiday and some restaurants close, it's a good time to go because everything is quieter.

TIME

Italy is one hour ahead of London, six hours ahead of New York and nine hours ahead of Los Angeles.

	JAN	FEB	MAR	APR	MAY	JUN	JUL	AUG	SEP	OCT	NOV	DEC
	50°F	52°F	59°F	64°F	73°F	79°F	84°F	82°F	79°F	70°F	57°F	54°F
	10°C	11°C	15°C	18°C	23°C	26°C	29°C	28°C	26°C	21°C	14°C	12°C

AVERAGE DAILY MAXIMUM TEMPERATURES

Spring (March to May) is a good time to visit if you want to avoid the summer heat.
Summer (June to August) can be extremely hot and humid, sometimes uncomfortably so in July and August.
Autumn (September to November) is generally the wettest time in Tuscany, and thunderstorms are common in September.
Winter (December to February) temperatures are often similar to those in northern European countries, and rainfall can be high.

WHAT'S ON

January *Pitti Immagine:* Fashion shows at the Fortezza da Basso.
February *Carnevale:* A low-key version of Venice's annual extravaganza.
March *Festa dell'Annunziata* (25 Mar): Traditionally the Florentine new year, with a fair to celebrate in Piazza Santissima Annunziata.
Scoppio del Carro: The Easter Sunday service at the Duomo culminates in an exploding carriage full of fireworks.
April *Mostra Mercato Internazionale dell' Artigianato:* An international

arts and crafts festival in the Fortezza da Basso.
May *Maggio Musicale:* Florence's international music and dance festival.
Festa del Grillo (Sun after Ascension): Crickets are sold in cages, then released in the park of Le Cascine (▷ 98).
June *Calcio in Costume:* An elaborate soccer game between town districts, played in medieval costume in Piazza Santa Croce; preceded by a procession.
Festa di San Giovanni (24 Jun): Fireworks in Piazzale Michelangelo

(▷ 87) celebrate the feast of Florence's patron saint.
Estate Fiesolana (mid-Jun to Sep): A Fiesole arts festival.
September *Festa del Rificolona* (7 Sep): Children carry paper lanterns in Piazza Santissima Annunziata to honour the birth of the Virgin.
October *Amici della Musica* (Oct–Apr): Concerts. Tickets from Teatro della Pergola (☎ 055 226 4316).
November *Festival dei Popoli* (Nov–Dec): A film festival in the Odeon Cinehall (▷ 46), showing international films.

NEED TO KNOW PLANNING AHEAD

114

Useful Websites

www.enit.it
Florence is particularly well covered on the Italian Tourist Board website, with information on history, culture, events, accommodation and gastronomy, in several languages.

www.turismo.intoscana.it
Run by the Tuscan Regional Tourist Board, this site covers the whole region, including Florence.

www.comune.fi.it
Florence City Council site has good information in English. Its tourism, museum and art pages are always up-to-date, with some good links.

www.firenzeturismo.it
The official APT tourism site with plenty of useful information in English.

www.firenze.net
This Florence-based site, in Italian and English, has information on where to go and what to do, with good maps and plenty of links.

www.emmeti.it
Another Italy-based site, in Italian and English, with a good range of information and links for Florence. It is strong on local events and has an online hotel reservation service.

www.initaly.com
This lively US site is clearly run by passionate Italophiles and has excellent planning tips and sightseeing hints.

www.florence.hotelguide.net
www.florence.hotelsfinder.com
Useful online hotel booking sites for Florence and other Italian destinations.

www.firenzemusei.it
You can prereserve a timed entrance ticket, to avoid a long wait to the main Florentine museums, including the Uffizi, via this efficient site.

PRIME TRAVEL SITES

www.fodors.com
A complete travel-planning site. You can research prices and weather; book air tickets, cars and rooms; ask questions (and get answers) from fellow travellers; and find links to other sites.

www.trenitalia.com
The official site of the Italian State Railways.

www.weatheronline.co.uk/Italy.htm
Good three-day weather predictions.

INTERNET ACCESS

Florence is rapidly coming into the 21st-century with its online facilities. WiFi points can be found at the airport, Santa Maria Novella station, many hotels and specialized internet cafés including:

Internet Train
www.internettrain.it
➕ G5 ✉ Via dell'Oriuolo 40r ☎ 055 263 8968
🕐 Mon–Sat 10–10, Fri, Sun 3–9
➕ F6 ✉ Via Porta Rossa 38 ☎ 055 274 1037
🕐 Mon–Sat 9.30am–midnight, Sun 10am–midnight
➕ F4 ✉ Via Guelfa 54–56 ☎ 055 212 204 🕐 Mon–Fri 9–8, Sat–Sun 11–10

More branches in the city.

Getting There

DIRECT FLIGHTS

There are no direct intercontinental flights to Florence so visitors have to fly to Milan (298km/185 miles north), Rome (277km/172 miles south) or another European city, then take a connecting flight or train. The flight from New York to Rome takes around nine hours; from the airport, take a shuttle train to Stazione Termini, then a train to Florence (2 hours).

ENTRY REQUIREMENTS

Check the latest passport and visa information before you travel; look up the British embassy website at www.gov.uk/government/world/italy or the United States embassy at www.usembassy.gov. EU citizens do not require visas to visit Italy.

CUSTOMS REGULATIONS

● EU nationals do not have to declare goods imported for their personal use.

● The limits for non-EU visitors are 200 cigarettes or 100 small cigars or 250g of tobacco; 1 litre of alcohol (over 22 per cent alcohol) or 2 litres of fortified wine; 60ml of perfume.

AIRPORTS

You can choose from three airports—Galileo Galilei Airport at Pisa, the small Amerigo Vespucci Airport at Florence and Guglielmo Marconi Airport at Bologna. The flight takes approximately 2 hours from London.

120km (75 miles)

Florence Airport
4km (2.5 miles) to central Florence
Bus, 20 minutes
€5

Bologna Airport
105km (65 miles) to Florence
Bus then train, 1 hour, around €14.50

Pisa Airport
80km (50 miles) to Florence
Train, 1 hour 15 minutes
€7.90

FROM FLORENCE AIRPORT

Amerigo Vespucci Airport (☎ 055 306 1300; www.aeroporto.firenze.it), also known as La Peretola, is 4km (2.5 miles) northwest of the city. It handles mainly domestic flights, with a limited number of daily departures to other European cities. There are two terminal buildings. The airport is connected to the main station (Autostazione Sita) in Florence by the light blue Volainbus shuttle (administered by ATAF and SITA ☎ 800 424 500; www.ataf.net), which runs every 30 minutes from 6am to 8.30pm, then every hour until 11.30pm. The journey takes 20 minutes and tickets, which cost €5, can be bought on board. Taxis cost around €20, plus possible surcharges (always check and agree a price before you set off).

FROM PISA AIRPORT

Pisa's Galileo Galilei Airport (☎ 050 849 300; www.pisa-airport.com) is the region's main point of entry 80km (50 miles) west of Florence, but with good road and train connections to the city. The one spacious terminal handles domestic and European flights. Five trains a day leave the airport for Florence

between 6.40am and around 10.20pm.
The journey takes about 75 minutes and
costs €7.90. Additional trains leave from Pisa
Centrale station; a shuttle bus runs every 30 to
40 minutes from the airport to the main train
station. Terravision (www.terravision.eu) runs an
airport bus transfer, taking around 70 minutes,
to Florence train station between 8.40am and
12.20am, costing €5 one way, €10 round-trip.
A taxi to Florence could cost you more than
€130. There is a helpful information office
inside the terminal where you can buy tickets
for trains and the bus.

FROM BOLOGNA AIRPORT

Guglielmo Marconi Airport (☎ 051 647 9615;
www.bologna-airport.it) is 105km (65 miles)
northeast of Florence in the Emilia-Romagna
region and handles a large volume of European
charter and scheduled flights, as well as budget
airline flights. A shuttle bus costing about €5
takes passengers to Bologna Centrale station
(www.grandistazioni.it). From here the journey
takes about an hour and costs around €10,
depending on type of train taken. Make sure
your ticket is valid for the right train. Rental cars
are available in Terminal A. Taxis to Florence
cost about €220.

ARRIVING BY TRAIN

The main station, Santa Maria Novella
(www.grandistazioni.it), has links with major
Italian cities as well as Paris, Ostend and
Frankfurt. Most buses in Florence depart from
the station forecourt, and there are usually taxis
waiting. Don't forget to validate your ticket, by
inserting it into the orange box on the platform,
before boarding your train.

ARRIVING BY LONG-DISTANCE BUS

Lazzi runs express services to and from Rome
and links Florence with major European cities
as part of the Eurolines network (✉ Piazza
della Stazione 3r ☎ 0573 193 7900;
www.lazzi.it).

Getting Around

STREET NUMBERS

One building can have two totally different numbers in Florence. The red system is for shops, restaurants and businesses; the blue system is for hotels or residences.

VISITORS WITH DISABILITIES

As in many other historic Italian cities, visitors with disabilities are far from well served in Florence, though things are improving. The official APT website (▷ 115) has detailed information for tourists with special needs. Many city museums are fully wheelchair-accessible, with ramps, elevators and suitable bathrooms. The grey and green buses can take wheelchairs, as does the electric D bus, which goes through the heart of Florence (board via the electric platform at the rear door). Taxis do take wheelchairs but it is wise to let them know when you make a reservation.

The Tuscan capital has no metro or subway system, but the historic area is largely traffic-free and can be crossed on foot in 30 minutes. There are conventional bus services, but no route is allowed to enter the traffic-free zone. These buses are useful, however, if you are staying on the outskirts of the city, or for getting around to the more outlying sights. In addition to the normal bus service there are four bus routes that do enter the traffic-free zone. Azienda Trasporti Area Fiorentina (ATAF) is responsible for public transportation in Florence (www.ataf.net).

BUSES

Bus routes in Florence are numbered and many start and end at the railway station at regular intervals. The zippy little electric buses that run through the traffic-free zone, identified by letters (C1–D), link all kinds of places in the narrow streets of the old city. Buy tickets at bars, tobacconists and from the ATAF booth on Piazza Stazione before boarding. Once on board, insert your ticket into the small orange box and it will be stamped with the time. Failure to validate your ticket can result in a hefty fine. The ticket is valid for the next 70 minutes for any bus; cost €1.20 or €2 if purchased on board. A multiple ticket gives you four 70-minute tickets; cost €4.70. The tourist information office by the station has bus maps.

HOP-ON-HOP-OFF BUS

If you really want to avoid any leg work, or want an overview of how the city is laid out, take an open-top bus ride with City Sightseeing (☎ 055 290 451; www.city-sightseeing.it). This bus permits visitors to get on and off at any number of designated stops on the tourist itinerary. The ticket is valid for 24 hours and costs €25.

LONG-DISTANCE BUS

There are three main bus companies in Florence: **Lazzi** ✉ Piazza della Stazione 3r ☎ 0573 193 7900; www.lazzi.it.

SITA serves the south and east region ✉ Via Santa Caterina da Siena 15r ☎ 800 373760 (in Italy only); www.sitabus.it.

CAP serves the region to the northeast of Florence, the Mugello ✉ Largo Fratelli Alinari 9 ☎ 055 214 637; www.capautolinee.it.

TAXIS

The official white Florentine taxis are clean and comfortable. You can hail them from central places such as the station or Piazza del Duomo, or call one of the official cab companies: Radio Taxi SO.CO.TA. (☎ 055 410 133) or Radio Taxi 4390 (☎ 055 4390). The meter starts running the moment your call is received. Supplements are charged for baggage and at night.

BICYCLES AND MOTORCYCLES

Bicycles can be rented from Florence by Bike ✉ Via San Zanobi 120–122r ☎ 055 488 992; www.florencebybike.it.

Mopeds and motorcycles can be rented from Alinari ✉ Via Zanobi 38r ☎ 055 280 500; www.alinarirental.com.

CARS

It is really not worth driving around Florence. Much of the city is closed to traffic, there is a one-way system and parking is difficult. However, a car is ideal if you plan to tour the surrounding Tuscan countryside. If you do rent a car, try to book a hotel with parking.

Main car rental companies are:

Avis ✉ Borgo Ognissanti 128r ☎ 055 213 629

Europcar ✉ Borgo Ognissanti 53–55r ☎ 055 290 438

Hertz Italiana ✉ Borgo Ognissanti 137 ☎ 055 239 8205

Tuscany's road system ranges from motorways (expressways) to winding lanes, and driving around outside the city is easy. Tolls are payable on highways (*autostrade*). Most, but by no means all, fuel stations take credit cards.

Highway emergency/Breakdown service (ACI): ☎ 803 116

Essential Facts

PRESS
● The Florentines preferred newspaper is *La Nazione*, a national paper produced in Florence.
● You can buy foreign newspapers and magazines at the station and at Sorbi, the kiosk in Piazza della Signoria.

MONEY
The euro is the official currency of Italy. Bank notes come in denominations of 5, 10, 20, 50, 100, 200 and 500 euros, and coins in denominations of 1, 2, 5, 10, 20 and 50 cents and 1 and 2 euros.

10 euros

50 euros

200 euros

500 euros

ELECTRICITY
● Voltage is 220 volts and sockets take two round pins.

EMERGENCY TELEPHONE NUMBERS
● Police ☎ 113; 112 (Carabinieri)
● Fire ☎ 115
● Ambulance ☎ 118
● State Police headquarters ✉ Via Zara 2 ☎ 055 49771

LOST PROPERTY
● Lost property office ✉ Via Veracini 5 ☎ 055 334 802 🕐 Mon–Wed, Fri–Sat 9–12.
● Report losses of passports to the police and other items to the Questura at Via Zara 2 ☎ 055 49771.
● Lost property office at the station ✉ Stazione Santa Maria Novella ☎ 055 235 6120 🕐 Daily 4.15pm–1.30am.

MAIL
● Main post office ✉ Via Pellicceria 3 ☎ 055 273 6481 🕐 Mon–Sat 8.15–7; www.poste.it.
● There is another big post office at ✉ Via Pietrapiana 53–55 ☎ 055 267 4231 🕐 Mon–Fri 8.15–7, Sat 8.15–12.30.
● Stamps (*francobolli*) can be purchased from post offices or from tobacconists displaying a white T sign on a black or blue background.
● Post boxes are small, red and marked 'Poste' or 'Lettere'. The slot on the left is for addresses within the city and the slot on the right is for other destinations.

MEDICINES AND MEDICAL TREATMENT
● EU nationals receive reduced-cost medical treatment on production of the relevant document (EHIC card for Britons). Private medical insurance for UK and all other nationals is still advised.
● Medical emergencies ☎ 118.
● Tourist medical service: has English-speaking doctors also available for call-outs ✉ Via Lorenzo il Magnifico 59 ☎ 055 475 411

🕐 Mon–Fri 11am–midnight, 5–6am,
Sat 11am–midnight; no appointment needed.
● Hospital: Santa Maria Nuova ✉ Piazza Santa
Maria Nuova 1 ☎ 055 69381.
Interpreters can be arranged for free through
Ospedale di Careggi (surgical accident and
emergency unit) ✉ Viale Pieraccini 17 ☎ 055
794 111; 055 794 7057; also dental services
☎ 055 794 7401 🕐 Mon–Sat 8.30–12.30.
● Pharmacies are indicated by a large green
or red cross. For pharmacy information ☎ 800
420 707 (toll-free from within Italy).
● All-night pharmacies:
Comunale 13 della Stazione ✉ At train station
☎ 055 216 761;
All'Insegna del Moro-Taverna ✉ Piazza San
Giovanni 20r ☎ 055 211 343;
Molteni ✉ Via dei Calzaiuoli 7r ☎ 055 289
490.

MONEY AND CREDIT CARDS
● Credit cards are widely accepted.
● ATMs are now plentiful.

NATIONAL HOLIDAYS
● **1 Jan:** New Year's Day; **6 Jan:** Epiphany;
Easter Sunday; Easter Monday; **25 Apr:**
Liberation Day; **1 May:** Labour Day; **15 Aug:**
Assumption; **1 Nov:** All Saints' Day; **8 Dec:**
Immaculate Conception; **25 Dec:** Christmas
Day; **26 Dec:** St. Stephen's Day.

TOILETS
● Italian toilets are generally
improving both in cleanliness
and facilities.
● Expect to pay about €1
for toilets. Those away from
the main tourist areas are
usually free.
● There are 22 public toilets
in Piazza San Giovanni, near
the Baptistery.
● Most bars and cafés have
toilets and usually allow
anybody to use them
(although it's polite to have
at least a drink).
● Florence has promoted
the initiative 'Courtesy Point'
in which several bars and
cafés have made their
toilets available to the
public.

CONSULATES
British Consulate	✉ Lungarno Corsini 2 ☎ 055 284 133
US Consulate	✉ Lungarno Amerigo Vespucci 38 ☎ 055 266 951

PLACES OF WORSHIP
Anglican	St. Mark's ✉ Via Maggio 16–18 ☎ 055 294 764
American Episcopal Church	St. James' ✉ Via Rucellai 9 ☎ 055 294 417
Lutheran	✉ Lungarno Torrigiani 11 ☎ 055 234 2775
Synagogue	✉ Via Farini 4 ☎ 055 245 252
Russian Orthodox	✉ Via Leone X 8 ☎ 055 490 148
Mosque	✉ Via Borgo Allegri 64–66r

ETIQUETTE

● Make the effort to speak some Italian: It will be appreciated.
● Shake hands on introduction and on leaving; once you know people better you can replace this with a kiss on each cheek.
● Use the polite form, *lei*, unless the other person uses *tu*.
● Always say *buon giorno* (hello) and *arrivederci* (goodbye) in shops.
● Italians do not get drunk in public.
● Smoking is banned in enclosed public places.

PRECAUTIONS

● Take care of wallets, handbags and backpacks as pickpockets target tourists.
● Keep the receipts and numbers of your traveller's cheques separately from the traveller's cheques.
● Keep a copy of the front page of your passport.
● List the numbers and expiration dates of your credit cards and keep the list separately.
● If a theft occurs, make a statement (*denuncia*) at a police station within 24 hours if you wish to make an insurance claim.
● After dark avoid Le Cascine and the station.

OPENING TIMES

● Banks: generally 8.30–3; in some instances also 2.45–4 Mon–Fri.
● Post offices: Mon–Fri 8.15–1.30, Sat 8.15–12.30.
● Shops: normally 8.30–1 and from 3 or 4 until 7 or 8; or 10–7.
● Museums: see individual entries.
● Churches: 7 or 8–12.30 and then from between 3 and 4 until 7.30. Main tourist attractions often stay open longer. No two are the same.

TELEPHONES

● Public phones are silver and orange. There is a phone centre known as Il Cairo, which includes internet access ✉ Via de' Macci 90r ☎ 055 263 8272 🕐 Mon–Sat 9.30–9, Sun 3–7.
● Few public telephones take coins. Phone cards (*carta* or *scheda* or *tessera telefonica*) are the most practical way to use a public phone.
● Directory Enquiries ☎ 1254.
● International directory enquiries ☎ 176. International operator ☎ 170; you can also make reverse charge international calls on this number via the operator.
● Cheap rate is all day Sunday and 9pm–8am (national) on other days; 10pm–8am (international).
● To call Italy from the UK, dial 00 followed by 39 (the code for Italy) then the number. To call the UK from Italy dial 00 44 then drop the first zero from the area code.
● To call Italy from the US dial 011 followed by 39. To call the US from Italy dial 00 1.
● Florence's area code (055) must always be dialled even if you are calling from within Florence.

TOURIST INFORMATION OFFICE

● Principal tourist office ✉ Via Cavour 1r ☎ 055 290 832/3; fax 055 276 0383; www.firenzeturismo.it.

Language

Italian pronunciation is totally consistent. Cs and gs are hard when they are followed by an a, o or u (as in 'cat' and 'got'), and soft if followed by an e or an i (as in 'child' or 'geranium'). The Tuscans often pronounce their cs and chs as hs.

USEFUL WORDS AND PHRASES

buon giorno	good morning
buona sera	good afternoon/ evening
buona notte	good night
ciao	hello/ goodbye (informal)
arrivederci	goodbye (informal)
arrivederla	goodbye (formal)
per favore	please
grazie	thank you
prego	you're welcome
come sta/stai?	how are you?
sto bene	I'm fine
mi dispiace	I'm sorry
scusi/scusa	excuse me/ I beg your pardon
permesso	excuse me (in a crowd)
quant'è?	how much is it?
quando?	when?
avete...?	do you have...?
qui/qua	here

EMERGENCIES

aiuto!	help!
dov'è il telefono più vicino?	where is the nearest telephone?
c'è stato un incidente	there has been an accident
chiamate la polizia	call the police
chiamate un medico/ un'ambulanza	call a doctor/ an ambulance
pronto soccorso	first aid
dov'è l'ospedale più vicino?	where is the nearest hospital?

BASIC VOCABULARY

sì	yes
no	no
non ho capito	I do not understand
sinistra	left
destra	right
entrata	entrance
uscita	exit
aperto	open
chiuso	closed
buono	good
cattivo	bad
grande	big
piccolo	small
con	with
senza	without
più	more

NUMBERS

uno/primo	1/first
due/secondo	2/second
tre/terzo	3/third
quattro/ quarto	4/fourth
cinque/quinto	5/fifth
sei	6
sette	7
otto	8
nove	9
dieci	10
venti	20
cinquanta	50
cento	100
mille	1,000
milione	1,000,000

Timeline

1115 The first comune (city state) is formed. Florence is run by a 100-strong assembly.

1250–60 The Primo Popolo regime controls Florence, dominated by trade guilds.

1296 The building of the Duomo begins, under Arnolfo di Cambio.

1340s Florence faces economic crisis after Edward III of England bankrupts the Peruzzi and Bardi and the Black Death plague halves the population.

1378 The uprising of the *ciompi* (wool carders) is the high point of worker unrest.

1406 Florence captures Pisa, gaining direct access to the sea.

1458 Cosimo de' Medici is recognized as ruler of Florence.

1469–92 Lorenzo the Magnificent rules.

1494 Florence surrenders to Charles VIII of France. Savonarola, a zealous monk, takes control of the city.

1498 Savonarola is burned at the stake after four years of rule, and Florence becomes a republic.

1502 The Republic of Florence retakes Pisa.

1570 Cosimo I creates a Tuscan state free from the Holy Roman Empire.

1743 Anna Maria Luisa, last of the Medici, dies. Florence is then ruled by the house of Lorraine under Francis Stephen.

1799–1814 Tuscany is occupied by Napoleon's troops.

1865–70 Florence becomes the capital of Italy. King Vittorio Emanuele is installed in the Pitti Palace.

1944 On 4 August, Germans blow up all the bridges in Florence with the exception of the Ponte Vecchio.

1966 The River Arno bursts its banks: Florence is flooded, the waters reaching to more than 6.5m (22ft) in some areas.

1993 The Uffizi Gallery is bombed.

2004 Michelangelo's *David* is unveiled after controversial restoration.

2010 Annual visitor numbers to Florence (population 400,000) topped the six million mark.

2013 Italian general elections resulted in stalemate, with many Florentines supporting the protest party *Movimento 5 Stelle* (5 Star Movement) led by comedian Beppe Grillo.

FAMOUS FLORENTINES

The poet Dante Alighieri, author of the *Divine Comedy*, was born in Florence in 1265. He was exiled from the city in 1302 because of his sympathies with the White Guelphs, and died in 1321.

Michelangelo Buonarroti (1475–1564) created some of his most famous works in Florence, including the sculpture *David*. Born in Caprese, he was buried in Florence's Santa Croce.

Political philosopher Niccolò Machiavelli was born in Florence in 1469.

Galileo Galilei (1564–1642), from Pisa, spent much of his life in Florence as the Medici court mathematician.

From far left: Bust of Cosimo di Giovanni de' Medici and on his horse; Napoleon Bonaparte; Dante Alighieri; fleur-de-lys guild emblem; the defensive Forte di Belvedere

Index

INDEX

Published by AA Publishing, a trading name of AA Media Limited, whose
registered office is Fanum House, Basing View, Basingstoke, Hampshire
RG21 4EA. Registered number 06112600.

© **AA Media Limited 2015**
First published 1997
New edition 2015

WRITTEN BY Susannah Perry
ADDITIONAL WRITING Jackie Staddon and Hilary Weston
UPDATED BY Sally Roy
SERIES EDITOR Clare Ashton
COVER DESIGN Tracey Freestone, Nick Johnston
DESIGN WORK Tracey Freestone
IMAGE RETOUCHING AND REPRO Ian Little

Colour separation by AA Digital Department
Printed and bound by Leo Paper Products, China

A CIP catalogue record for this book is available from the British Library.

ISBN 978-0-7495-7622-6

A05237
Maps in this title produced from mapping © MAIRDUMONT / Falk Verlag 2012
Transport map © Communicarta Ltd, UK

The Automobile Association would like to thank the following photographers and companies for their assistance in the preparation of this book.

1 AA/J Tims; 2–18t AA/Simon McBride; 4cl AA/Simon McBride; 5c AA/Ken Paterson; 6cl AA/Simon McBride; 6cc AA/Clive Sawyer; 6cr AA/Simon McBride; 6bl AA/Terry Harris; 6bc AA/Ken Paterson; 6br AA/Simon McBride; 7cl AA/J Edmanson; 7cr AA/Simon McBride; 7bl AA/Clive Sawyer; 7br AA/Simon McBride; 10ctr AA/Simon McBride; 10cr AA/Simon McBride; 10cbr AA/Terry Harris; 10br AA/J Tims; 11ctl AA/Terry Harris; 11cbl AA/Ken Paterson; 11bl AA/J Tims; 13ctl AA/Clive Sawyer; 13cl AA/Terry Harris; 13cbl AA/Clive Sawyer; 13bl AA/Terry Harris; 14ctr AA/Max Jourdan; 14cr AA/J Tims; 14cbr AA/Ken Paterson; 14br AA/Terry Harris; 16ctr AA/Simon McBride; 16cbr AA/Ken Paterson; 16br AA/Simon McBride; 17ctl AA/Simon McBride; 17cl AA/Simon McBride; 17cbl AA/Clare Garcia; 17bl AA/Terry Harris; 18ctr AA/Clive Sawyer; 18cr Photodisc; 18cbr AA/Clive Sawyer; 18br AA/ Clive Sawyer; 19t AA/Simon McBride; 19ct AA/Ken Paterson; 19cb AA/Richard Ireland; 19b AA/Terry Harris; 20/21 AA/Clive Sawyer; 24l AA/Clive Sawyer; 24/25t AA/Clive Sawyer; 24/25c AA/Simon McBride; 25tr AA/J Edmanson; 25cl AA/Ken Paterson; 25c AA/Ken Paterson; 25cr AA/Ken Paterson; 26l AA/Simon McBride; 26r Santa Croce, Florence, Giraudon/Bridgeman Art Library; 27l AA/James Tims; 27r Scala, Florence 2006; 28l AA/Simon McBride; 28c AA/Simon McBride; 28r AA/ Simon McBride; 29l AA/Simon McBride; 29r AA/Clive Sawyer; 30tl AA; 30/31t AA/Simon McBride; 30c AA/Simon McBride; 30/31c AA/Terry Harris; 31tr AA/ Simon McBride; 31cr AA/Simon McBride; 32l AA/J Tims; 32c AA/J Tims; 32r AA/J Edmanson; 33 AA/Simon McBride; 34t AA/Simon McBride; 34cl AA/Terry Harris; 34c AA/Clive Sawyer; 34cr AA/Clive Sawyer; 35 AA/Terry Harris; 36l AA/J Tims; 36c AA/Terry Harris; 36r AA/J Tims; 37-39t AA/Simon McBride; 37bl AA/Ken Paterson; 37br AA/Clive Sawyer; 38bl AA/Clive Sawyer; 38br AA/Clive Sawyer; 39bl AA/ Simon McBride; 39br AA/Clive Sawyer; 40 AA/Terry Harris; 41t AA/Simon McBride; 42t AA/Simon McBride; 43t AA/Simon McBride; 44t AA/Simon McBride; 45 AA/ Terry Harris; 46t AA/Terry Harris; 47t AA/Eric Meacher; 48t AA/Simon McBride; 49t AA/Clive Sawyer; 50t AA/Ken Paterson; 51 AA/Simon McBride; 54 AA/Clive Sawyer; 55 AA/Simon McBride; 56l AA/Simon McBride; 56c AA/Simon McBride; 56r AA/Ken Paterson; 57l AA/Terry Harris; 57r AA/Terry Harris; 58tl AA/Simon McBride; 58tr AA/Clive Sawyer; 58cl AA/Ken Paterson; 58cr AA/Simon McBride; 59t AA/Simon McBride; 59cl AA/Simon McBride; 59cr AA/J Edmanson; 60 Galleria dell' Accademia, Florence/Bridgeman Art Library; 60/61 Raffaello Bencini/Alinari Archives, Florence; 61r AA/Simon McBride; 62l AA/Simon McBride; 62r AA/J Tims; 63l AA/Simon McBride; 63r AA/Simon McBride; 64l AA/Terry Harris; 64r AA/Terry Harris; 65l AA/Simon McBride; 65r AA/Simon McBride; 66l AA/Simon McBride; 66c AA/Clive Sawyer; 66r AA/J Edmanson; 67l AA/Clive Sawyer; 67r AA/Terry Harris; 68-69t AA/Ken Paterson; 68b AA/Simon McBride; 69bl AA/Terry Harris; 69br AA/C Sawyer; 70t AA/Terry Harris; 71t AA/Terry Harris; 72t AA/Simon McBride; 73t AA/ Simon McBride; 74t Digitalvision; 75t AA/Simon McBride; 76t AA/Terry Harris; 77 AA/Clive Sawyer; 80 AA/J Tims; 81 AA/Simon McBride; 82l AA/Ken Paterson; 82r AA/Clive Sawyer; 83l AA/Clive Sawyer; 83r AA/Simon McBride; 84t AA/Simon McBride; 84c AA/J Tims; 84/85 AA/J Edmanson; 86-87t AA/Ken Paterson; 86bl AA/Simon McBride; 86br AA/Clive Sawyer; 87b AA/Simon McBride; 88t AA/Terry Harris; 89t AA/Ken Paterson; 90t AA/Simon McBride; 91t AA/Digitalvision; 91c AA/ Terry Harris; 92t AA/Terry Harris; 93 AA/Terry Harris; 96 AA/J TimsSeat Archive/ Alinari Archives; 97l AA/C Sawyer; 97r AA/T Harris; 98t AA/Ken Paterson; 98b The Bridgeman Art Library; 99t AA/Ken Paterson; 99bl AA/Terry Harris; 99br AA/Terry Harris; 100t AA/Ken Paterson; 100b AA/Simon McBride; 101t AA/Simon McBride; 102t AA/Michelle Chaplow; 103t Digitalvision; 104t Photodisc; 105t AA/Clive Sawyer; 106t David Wasserman/brandxpictures; 107 AA/Clive Sawyer; 108-112t AA/ Clive Sawyer; 108ctr AA/J Edmanson; 108cr AA/Clive Sawyer; 108cbr AA/Simon McBride; 108br AA/Terry Harris; 113 AA/Terry Harris; 114-125t AA/Terry Harris; 118b AA/J Tims; 120 ECB; 124bl AA/Clive Sawyer; |124bc AA/Clive Sawyer; |124bc AA; 124br AA/Clive Sawyer; 125bl AA/Clive Sawyer; 125br AA/Simon McBride.

Every effort has been made to trace the copyright holders, and we apologise in advance for any accidental errors. We would be happy to apply the corrections in the following edition of this publication.

Titles in the Series